Ignazio Somis

A True and Particular Account of three Women who Were Buried

Thirty-Seven Day's

Ignazio Somis

A True and Particular Account of three Women who Were Buried Thirty-Seven Day's

ISBN/EAN: 9783337258108

Printed in Europe, USA, Canada, Australia, Japan

Cover: Foto ©ninafisch / pixelio.de

More available books at **www.hansebooks.com**

A TRUE AND PARTICULAR
ACCOUNT,
OF THE

Moſt Surpriſing PRESERVATION,

AND

HAPPY DELIVERANCE,

OF

Three WOMEN who were BURIED, Thirty-Seven Day's, in the RUINS of a STABLE, by a heavy Fall of SNOW, from the Mountains, at the Village of *Bergemoletto*, in *Italy*.

With CURIOUS REMARKS.

BY IGNAZIO SOMIS,

Profeſſor of Phyſic in the Univerſity of TURIN, and Phyſician to his Sardinian Majeſty.

TRANSLATED FROM THE ITALIAN.

LONDON,

Printed for H. SERJEANT, at the BLACK-SWAN, without TEMPLE-BAR, 1768.

Price Bound, Three Shillings.

TO HIS

SACRED MAJESTY

CHARLES EMMANUEL

King of SARDINIA, &c.

IGNAZIO SOMIS.

I MOST humbly prefent to your facred Majefty a compofition, which derives its fole merit from that important commiffion, with which you were pleafed to honour me, me, at the time when you moſt gracioully reſigned your invaluable health to my care. And can there be an object more dear and more ſacred to thoſe people, whom heaven has bleſſed with the happineſs of living under a government, ſo conſpicuous for the moſt impartial adminiſtration of juſtice, together with a diſplay of that wiſdom, by which king's reign, and the mighty are rulers of the earth? The whole world knows with, what a

benign

benign afpect, your majefty amidft the other moft weighty concerns of this happy ftate, looks down on the arts and fciences, which have made fo flourifhing a figure ever fince your aufpicious reign. Juftly then may a faithful fubject hope, that fince he has been fo fortunate as to be appointed in this Royal Univerfity, to the honourable poft of cultivating thofe arts, fo dear to your Majefty, you will condefcend to accept of this little performance,

ance, which with the profoundest respect, I dedicate to your Majesty, to whom it owes its existence, begging you will take it together with the author under your august patronage.

ADVERTISEMENT.

THE tranflator has no occafion to mention any thing by way of preface to the following performance. Its reputation is fufficiently eftablifhed, not only in Italy, but likewife in England, where it has met with the higheft approbation. He only begs the indulgence of the public for the liberty he has taken, in retaining a few words from the Italian, as *Valanca*, *Forefta*, for want of proper terms in Englifh to exprefs their fignification.

BOOKS printed for T. OSBORNE.

Having purchased the remaining Copies of the following beautiful and elegant Work, of which there are but few left, now offers them to the Public, at the easy Expences of 1l. 16s. elegantly bound, formerly sold for 3l. 3s. in Sheets. There are a few Copies on Royal Paper, Price 2l. 2s. elegantly bound.

SPENCER's FAIRY QUEEN,

IN Three Volumes Royal Quarto, one of the best printed Books in England. With an exact Collation of the two original Editions published by himself. To which is now added a new Life of the Author, by THOMAS BIRCH, D. D. Secretary to the Royal Society. Together with a Glossary.

This Edition is adorned with Thirty-two Copper-plates (not in any other Edition) from the original Drawing of the late William Kent, Esq; Architect and principal Painter to his Majesty, which cost upwards of One Thousand Pounds.—What Copies remain unsold will be advanced to the original Price.

Now published, carefully revised and improved, a New Edition, elegantly printed on a new Letter, and fine Paper, Pr. 3s. bound. Dedicated by Permission to the NOBLEMEN and GENTLEMEN educated a MARYBONE School,

THE NEW
ART of LETTER-WRITING,
Divided into two Parts.

I. Containing Rules and Directions for writing Letters on all Sorts of Subjects.

With a Variety of Examples, equally elegant and instructive.

II. A Collection of Letters on the most interesting Occasions in Life.

Wherein are inserted the proper Methods of addressing Persons of all Ranks; some necessary Orthographical Directions; the Forms of Messages for Cards; and Thoughts upon a Diversity of Subjects.

The whole composed on a Plan intirely new; chiefly calculated for the Instruction of Youth, but may be of singular Service to Gentlemen, Ladies, and all others, who are desirous to attain the true Style and Manner of a polite Epistolary Intercourse.

By a Gentleman of Fortune, for his own Amusement, and the Instruction of his Children.

N. B. This Work is an intire new Performance, and there has been so great a Demand for it, that some Thousands have been sold off in less than these twelve Months past.

☞ Be pleased to order this New Art of Letter-writing.

※ There is a remarkable Letter in this Work relating to Matrimony.

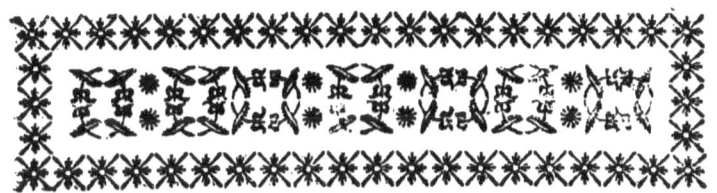

A N

ESSAY, &c.

IN the present age, there is not, I suppose, any one to be found, who, having cultivated the natural sciences, and read such authors, as have contributed to carry them to that height, which they now enjoy, is not thoroughly persuaded of this great truth, that the safest and easiest way to exalt them to their zenith, is first to make oneself thoroughly acquainted with what has been already discovered by industrious, attentive, and exact observers, and then to add to this knowledge new, diligent, and repeated experiments.

experiments. In fact, difficult as it may be to attend more to the naked truth of things, than to the authority of those who speak of them, and to forget those maxims which we have, as it were, sucked in with our milk; yet we may observe, that those opinions, which formerly had taken deep and firm root in the minds of philosophers, and became interwoven, in a manner, with their frame and constitution, are now become stale and obsolete, to the great advantage of true philosophy. Such are these, that we ought blindly to swallow every thing delivered by those, who for many ages have tyrannized in the schools of philosophy, and triumphantly drawn after them the brightest geniuses; that we should never scruple peremptorily to assign certain principles, by which all the operations of nature, within our observation, may be explained; that to confess ingenuously our not being able to discover sure and solid reasons for every thing, is highly unbecoming a philosopher; with others of the

the same stamp. So that whoever should unhappily let any of them escape him, might deservedly expect the following reply of the Florentine poet.

"What! you imperiously require
"That I should fetter my understanding,
"And not let it range farther than you can
"see it.
"Whoever gives himself any trouble a-
"bout these trifles,
"No longer can be said to aim at truth;
"But wants to keep up the value of these
"jewels,
"Which being false, expose the wearer
"to the contempt of him
"Who wears true ones, and are them-
"selves brought into disrepute
"By being compared with those of real
"value."

Wherefore, the lovers of truth and wisdom, fully persuaded that we are not blindly to follow the opinion of others, nor to devise and invent reasons for things, but to examine every work of nature with a clear and penetrating eye, have laid it down as a maxim, built upon experience, that to investigate the causes of any particular phenomenon, we should be first certain of the existence of such phenomenon; and that there is no attaining such certainty, without observing all the most minute circumstances, which establish that existence, and let us into the nature of the thing itself. What judgment could a man form of the bodies which surround us, and so beautifully adorn the universe with their different colours, whose organs of sight were so vitiated, as not to be susceptible of the images formed by the rays of light flowing from them. We hear, and we read that seamen can easily discover, at forty miles distance, especially by night, the shores of Spain, Ceylon, Sumatra, and other countries, merely by the different odours emitted by those countries; a degree of acuteness those must never pretend to, in whom, through any dis-

order

order or defect in their organs of smelling, the very subtil particles exhaled by odorous bodies cannot excite the precise kind of motion necessary to produce such a sensation. The same may be said of the other senses, concerning which, as well as the proper objects of them, those, in whom the respective organs are not found and perfect, must not pretend to judge. To reason, therefore, with success upon any subject, it is first necessary to ascertain, by exact observation, all the properties belonging to it; and he, who shall have thus ascertained most of these properties, may, by comparing them together, expect to see farthest into the rest. Hence it is evident, that to philosophize with judgment, nothing is so indispensably requisite, as observation and experiment, to which, however, we are not to refuse the assistance of our reason, when the subject will admit of it.

It was by this resplendent light that Galileo, Torricelli, Bacon, Boyle, and Newton, not to mention many other able

able and illuftrious philofophers, directed all their inquiries, boldly leaving the footfteps of thofe who went before them, who were for deciding every queftion, and explaining every phenomenon by vain and groundlefs hypothefes. They, on the contrary, foberly fat down to confider and examine, with the greateft caution and circumfpection, the works of nature in every light in which they could be confidered and examined, whereby they difcovered a vaft country, and opened a direct and fecure road to the golden manfions of pure and genuine truth. This light foon diffufed itfelf over all the other fciences, which either derive their origin from phyfics, or are intimately and indiffolubly connected with them. Nor is this all, for thefe fciences have acquired a new afpect, and received confiderable encreafe and improvement from the many obfervations and experiments made upon their immediate objects. How much, for inftance, is not natural hiftory indebted to the great diligence

gence and experimental inveſtigation of the incomparable Malpighi, whoſe name will flouriſh in the minds of men, while there remains in them the leaſt fondneſs for noble and uſeful knowledge. What a great revolution has been brought about in the theory of medicine, by the important obſervation of Hervey to aſcertain the circulation of the blood, barely hinted at by thoſe who went before him. The theory of reſpiration has been greatly illuſtrated by the obſervations of Swammerdam, upon which new light has been ſince thrown by the famous Haller, to whom medical hiſtory, anatomy, phyſiology, and every other branch of the healing art are ſo much indebted. Who would have thought, that almoſt all bodies are phoſphorous, if that diligent and indefatigable experimenter, Beccari, had not evidently proved it by repeated obſervations. I ſhall not mention many other great men of Italy, England, France, and other countries, who in the paſt and the preſent centuries, have, to their own immortal honour, and the unspeakable advantage of those engaged in such studies, most carefully observed and examined some one subject, and some another, and by means of such observation, happily placed them in that point of light to which the weakness of human understanding is allowed to aspire.

It is intirely to the desire of coming at truth by such methods, that we are to attribute the institution and flourishing condition of those glorious and renowned assemblies of able and learned men in so many cities of Europe, I mean their academies. These great men, accustomed never to trust the eyes of others, nor even their own, till they had observed, and tried, and again tried and observed, began towards the middle of the seventeenth century to assemble together in Florence; and at length, animated by the princely liberalities and munificence of prince Leopold, afterwards cardinal of Medicis, and of the great duke Ferdinand II, both admirers and

and patrons of the sciences and fine arts, instituted the academy del Cimento. In 1667, they published *i saggi di naturali esperienze*, written with singular chastity and elegance of stile, by count Lorenzo Magalotti, and lately translated into Latin, by that learned Dutchman Musschenbrock, which will remain to latest posterity so many testimonies of Italian diligence, penetration, and precision, in making experiments. And indeed there is seldom any thing more wanting, to leave the Italian geniuses no room to envy other nations, than an exemption from the drudgeries of common life, and such further rewards and encouragements as might make them exert those singular talents bestowed on them by providence, and indefatigably aspire to great things. In the same manner, and nearly at the same time, with the academy of Cimento, started up in England the Royal Society, in Paris the Royal Academy of Sciences, in Germany that of the *Curiosi Naturæ*, the academies of Berlin, Upfal, Petersburgh, and Gottingen. These were followed, in the beginning of the present century, by our Institute and academy of Bologna. An ardent thirst for knowledge brought together in the house of doctor Sandri, the following learned men, viz. Stancari, Morgagni, the three Eustachios, and the two Manfredis, a family no less qualified than that of the three Zanottis, to render their country illustrious; a taste and genius for learning being so natural to them, that even the women have excelled in the mathematics or belles lettres. The fame of this assembly, soon made its way over the Alps, and these bright and penetrating geniuses were taken notice of by a nobleman, fond of the sciences, and zealous for the honour of his country, who requested them, to the great concern of doctor Sandri, to make use of his house, and meet there some days in every week, as they might be able more conveniently to confer with each other, and communicate their observations, and discoveries.

difcoveries. This happened in 1705. This nobleman was count Marfigli, known to the republic of letters by his expenfive works, which prove him to have been a man of uncommon parts and learning, efpecially in natural hiftory. The count, unwilling that fuch ufeful difcoveries, made in his own houfe, fhould any longer remain in obfcurity, prevailed on the pope, and the fenate of Bologna, to patronize and promote an inftitution, which fo indefatigably cultivated the fciences. The confequence was that the inftitute was erected and eftablifhed in 1712, and opened for the firft time with a great concourfe of all ranks, the thirteenth of March in the year 1714. So learned an academy, furely, will never forget the fplendid magnificence of that nobleman, who beftowed upon it a very large and moft valuable collection of natural curiofities, with inftruments and machines made by him in his extenfive travels, and brought together with infinite expence. I have often had an account

count of this happy eſtabliſhment, from my moſt amiable maſter the Abate Gerolamo Tagliazucchi, who was not only a profound mathematician and philoſopher, and an excellent orator and poet, but likewiſe a zealous and indefatigable promoter of the ſciences and polite arts. Whoever knows what gratitude is, muſt readily conceive how bitterly I do and ſhall always regret the irreparable loſs of ſo great a man, who with unſpeakable goodneſs and affection attended to my education for eighteen years together, guiding me up the ſteep paths of thoſe ſciences, which himſelf poſſeſſed in a ſupreme degree. But I muſt not now indulge my deſire of doing juſtice to his merit. The time will come, and I hope it is not far off, in which I ſhall endeavour to let mankind know, how much they are indebted to him, by publiſhing the *collection of poems* promiſed by him, in the prefatory diſcourſe to his *collection of proſe writings for the uſe of the royal ſchools*, and all his other works;

moſt

moſt of them compoſed in the royal univerſity.

But to make an end of this digreſſion, occaſioned by the pleaſing remembrance of ſo good a maſter, the works continually iſſuing from theſe ſo illuſtrious academies, which have chiefly at heart the cultivation and improvement of phyſics, botany, anatomy, phiſiology, and medicine, evidently prove, that there is no road but that of experience and obſervation, by which a man can hope to make any progreſs in theſe ſciences, and attain any degree of true knowledge. And, not to dwell longer on the already mentioned branches of learning, it is certain that the medical hiſtories of uncommon diſeaſes, and ſuch ſingular caſes as there are few opportunities of obſerving, of which, however, we have now many volumes publiſhed by different perſons, (would to God, they had been all written with equal diligence and accuracy, and with leſs fondneſs for the marvellous than the truth) all tend, if we conſider them

with

with an equitable eye, to the fame laudable end. Among thefe fingular cafes, we may certainly venture to rank that I am now about to fpeak of; an event fo thoroughly furprifing in all its circumftances, that for my part, I may fafely affirm, I never heard or read of any thing like it.

It has hitherto been the almoft general opinion of philofophers, that the vapours and exhalations of earthly bodies, by whatever caufes (repeated experiments may perhaps difcover and determine them) carried into the atmofphere, afcend to different heights, on account of the different denfity, and confequently different fpecific gravity of the air at different diftances from the earth; and that, whenever thefe vapours or exhalations acquire a greater fpecific gravity than that of the air in which they float, they fall back towards the furface of the earth. This has hitherto been chiefly attributed either to the fun's early rays ftriking directly againft thefe vapours, and fo bearing them down to the earth: or to

their

their requiring more time to be heated, and confequently rarified by the fun's rays, than the circumambient air, which, as lighter, muft of courfe let them fall to the earth; a thing we may often obferve in fpring or autumn along rivers and other waters, which continue for fome time covered with a thick fog: or to the quantity of vapours already raifed into the atmofphere, as being fo great that new ones cannot find room enough to difperfe in it, and therefore meeting with a refiftance fuperior to that with which they are impelled: or to the vapours being of fuch different qualities, that they cannot mix without producing a kind of fermentative motion fufficient, as we may obferve in chemical operations, to precipitate fome of them: or elfe to the air fupporting the vapours, being fwept from under them by horizontal winds, and giving way to a rarer air, lefs qualified to fupport their bodies moving, as every one knows, towards that quarter in which they find the leaft refiftance: or

elfe

else to the winds blowing in an oblique direction towards the earth, and carrying the vapours with them in the same direction: or else, in fine, to their being driven one against another by opposite winds, or against hills and mountains, and thereby condensed so as to become heavier than the air itself. For, some of these causes, or, perhaps, others, which may be hereafter discovered by the exact observations of philosophers, destroying the equilibrium between the vapours floating in the air, and the air itself; it is evident that these vapours must fall back to the surface of the earth, and, in their fall, form, according to their weight, size, and figure; fog, rain, snow, or some other of these appearances, by the philosophers stiled aqueous meteors. Among the causes which make the earthly vapours mixed with the air, fall back to the earth, that of the winds driving them against the mountains, with which we are in a manner entirely surrounded, is, as far as we can hitherto guess, the most common cause in

this

this part of the world. And therefore we know that there falls more rain and fnow in the mountains, than in the flat country; rain, when there is not cold enough to freeze the vapours before they come near the earth; and fnow, whenever they mix with any of thofe particles capable of producing congelation, or the air itfelf is cold enough to have alone that effect. But as it is reafonable to believe, that the air of mountains is lefs warm than that of plains, hence it follows, that it muft oftener, and more heavily fnow on the former, than on the latter. Three years ago, at fix o'clock in the morning of the twenty-eighth of July, the fpirit of a Reaumeriau thermometer of mine, was but five degrees above the freezing point at the baths of Valdieri; and about five in the evening, when it had got up to eleven degrees, there fell for the fpace of half an hour, a frozen rain, which, all to its being a little more denfe, had the appearance of fnow; whereas in another thermometer of mine

at

at Turin, and the fellow to the firſt, the ſpirit roſe at the ſame time to twenty degrees, as appears from the notes taken by the perſon whom I had ordered to obſerve it in my abſence. The ſame thing had already happened about ſix in the evening of the twenty-ſecond, when the ſpirit of the thermometer at the bath, was at twelve; and that at Turin at twenty-ſeven degrees. On the ninth of June, of the year 1749, there fell in the valley of Demonte, and likewiſe in the town itſelf, ſo great a quantity of ſnow, that it covered the earth to the height of ſix of our inches. To this it is owing, that in the mountains the ſnow ſometimes falls in ſuch vaſt quantities, and accumulates to ſuch a degree, that when ariſen to a certain height, it falls into the lower grounds in immenſe heaps, which in our country are called *Valanche*, (a word derived from the French word *Lavange*) and which, perhaps, by the Tuſcans are called *Labine* or *Lavine*. This ſtate of the ſnow is not unlike
what

what the illustrious Tozzetti relates of heaps of stones, in his account of some journies made by him, through different parts of Tuscany. Describing, in his first tome, the valley of Buti, he thus speaks of the declivity called *Il Saſſeto*. " In order to understand the meaning of this word *Saſſeto*, it is proper to observe, that the sides of the Pisan mountains are generally so very sharp and steep, that the rain waters in their descent along them, acquire a surprising degree of velocity and strength. Besides, as those mountains are very high, and near the sea, the clouds easily stop on their summit, and almost instantaneously dissolve into cataracts, which tumbling headlong down the precipice, and every moment acquiring new bulk and strength, carry along with them, all the loose and single stones they meet with; and then by the dashing of these stones, and their own shock, root up all the fir and chesnut-trees they meet with, and roll through a great extent of country, a horrible quantity of

large

large stones, till the declivity decreasing, and consequently their own strength, they are obliged to leave them behind. These *Labine*, or vast heaps, which consist of nothing but stones (the earth being carried off to the bottom along with the water) are called Saffeti, and are very common in the Pisan mountains, especially in the valley of Calci, and are visible at a great distance, for they look like so many squares, or naked slips of ground in the midst of thick woods." The learned Scheuchzer, in order to display in his fourth journey over the Swifs alps, the great danger, to which persons travelling by mount Gottardo are exposed by these Valancas, begins by explaining the word itself, and says, " *Labinæ* vel *Labenæ*, vocabulum ad ultimam latinitatem relegandum notat nivof. s. ingentes moles conglomeratas, quæ per declivia Alpium latera *labi* (inde autem nomen) solent. Mihi cum Simlero de Alpibus, p. 113. videtur latina æque ac germanica denominatio arcessenda a Rhætis, qui

italico

italico idcomate labinas vocant *Lavine,* vernaculo autem *Lavigne.*" And thefe he reduces to two principal kinds, one of which, he fays, is called by the Italians *Lavina di freddo,* the other, *Lavina di caldo.* " Labinarum genera funt potiffimuum duo, unum, fi novæ, & molles duntaxat nives conglobantur, et labuntur. Simler p. 113. b. vocant has *Windlowenen,* tum a caufâ, vento nivem recens delapfam commovente, tum ob effectum,' quoniam celeriter ruunt, et lapfu fuo ventum procellofum excitant, qui etiam eminus quæque profternit, abietes craffifimas frangit, homines et jumenta fuffocat, ædes & ftabula fubvertit; item *Staublowinen,* Staubloweln (Rahm Gefpr. p. 132) a vento et pulvere nivofo, quo conftat, et quævis in valle obvia obtegit ac involvit; alji κατ' ἐξοχήν *Schneelauwinen,* quod ex mera nive conftant: Itali *Lavine di freddo,* Engadienfes *Lavigne da fraid,* quafi dicas *Labinas ex frigore, Labinas Hyemales,* hybernas; quoniam hyeme potiffimum, et frigidiffima aeris temperaturâ (qua nivei

flocci

flocci recens lapsi raram porosam con stituunt massam a vento quovis facile dissipabilem, nec dum propius coactam) oriri solent. Sunt hæ admodum periculosæ, eo scilicet sensu, quatenus fuga non tam facile evitari possunt, et cito sæpe viatores obruunt, nec via recta decurrunt, sed a vento flante nunc hac, nunc illac pelluntur; alio tamen respectu minus lethales, quam quæ mox describendæ veniunt, quoniam minus sunt compactæ, ut qui iis involvuntur facilius se extricare queant, nec vitam statim suffocati amittant." This first kind described by Scheuchzer is not, I think, called *Valanca* by our Alpineers, but *Tormenta*, a word taken from the French *Tourmente*, signifying properly snow whirled about with great impetuosity by the wind, which tears the thickest and stoutest trees from their roots, beats down animals to the ground, and suffocates them; as is too often the case with those who are indiscreet enough to attempt the passage of the *Colle di Tenda*, or Mount Cenis, at a time

time judged improper by thofe who continually refide in fuch fituations, and can therefore foretell, by certain figns, the fudden rife of thefe terrible whirlwinds. Of the fecond kind he writes thus: " Alterum pergit *Siml.* quod inveteratam nivem quoque trahit, et multum terræ fecum abripit. Nuncupantur hæ *Schlofs* et *Schlaglauwinen*, quoniam non tam fecundante vento, quam ponderofâ mole cuncta, quæ in via occurrunt, profternunt, diruunt, nec folam nivem fecum vehunt, fed et arbores radicitus extirpatas, rupes et faxa prægrandia; et viatores, quos corripiunt, vel ftatim fuffocant, vel tam arcte claudunt, ut capite folo liberi, reliquo autem corpore integro involuti fefe exolvere nequeunt, fed perire neceffum habeant. Hoc fane fenfu prioribus funt magis exitiales, minus tamen periculofæ, quatenus non tam cito defluunt, nec etiam tam latum occupant fpatium, quin mature confpectæ evitari poffint. Itali hoc labinarum genus vocant *Lavina di caldo*, Engadienfes *Lavigna da chiod*,

chiod, quoniam verno potiſſimum tempore, quo calor redit et nives conſtipat, excitari ſolent. Solent hæ delapſu ſuo ingentes concitare fragores, tonitrui ſimiles, ob concuſſam violenter terram, et repercuſſum ad latera montium aerem tremulum." Here with us, this ſecond kind is alone called *Valanca*; which word I muſt beg leave to uſe in relating an event that happened a few years ago in our neighbourhood.

It has been obſerved, that the *Valancas* of ſnow are formed two ſeveral ways. The firſt is, when the ſnow falls for ſome length of time, and in large quantities, on a plain, forming with the horizon, an angle of 45° or thereabouts, and heated to ſuch a degree, as little by little to melt that part of the ſnow which immediately covers it. For the whole body, it is plain, reſting on a ſurface too ſmooth and ſlippery to retain it, cannot but ſlide away, and tend downwards; ſo that, if by ſuch motion, it reaches a precipice, it muſt fall, and in conſequence of the impetus acquired by ſuch

such fall, continue to move and run even over any little horizontal plain it may meet with, till it meets with some resistance capable of effectually stopping it. It is in this manner, and for the very same reason, that often pretty large tracts of land, with the plants, trees, and sometimes even the houses upon them, get loose from the hills; when the earth in which they are fixed, is of such a consistence as to let the water through it in sufficient quantity to destroy its adhesion to the part immediately under it, and so move towards that side where the declivity is greatest; sliding, if the plane, upon which they move, makes with the horizon an angle less than 45°; and rolling and tumbling if it happens to be much greater. The other way, in which valancas are formed, is when the snow accumulates on a plain, making with the horizon an angle much greater than forty-five degrees, till the perpendicular, from its center of gravity, falling without the base, or its weight growing too great for the force with which it adheres to the ground, the whole, or a great part of it, suddenly gets loose, and rushing down violently, overturns every thing that opposes its headlong course. Now, it is but too often we have in our mountains, fatal instances of both these kinds of valancas. In the months of February and March of the year 1755, we had in Turin, a great fall of rain, the sky having been almost constantly overcast from the ninth of February, till the twenty-fourth of March. During this interval, in which, namely, on the thirteenth of February, the mercury fell to twenty-six inches and eight lines, and never rose to above twenty-seven inches and seven lines; it rained almost every day, but snowed only on the morning of the twenty-first of February, when the liquor of Reaumur's thermometer, stood but one degree above the freezing point. Now, as for the reasons already assigned, it often snows in the mountains, when it only rains in the plain; it cannot appear surprising,

that

that during this interval, there fell vast quantities of snow in the mountains that surround us, and in course, several valancas were formed. In fact, there happened so many in different places on the side of Aosta, Lanzo, Susa, Savoy, and the county of Nice, that by the end of March, no less than two hundred persons had the misfortune of losing their lives by them. Of these overwhelmed by these valancas, three persons, however, *Mary Anne Roccia Bruno*, *Anne Roccia*, and *Margaret Roccia*, had reason to think themselves, in other respects, extremely happy, having been dug alive on the twenty-fifth of April, out of a stable, under the ruins of which, they had been buried, the nineteenth of March, about nine in the morning, by a valanca of snow, forty two feet higher than the roof, to the incredible surprise of all those who saw them, and afterwards heard them relate how they lived all this while, with death, as we may say, continually staring them in the face.

The road from Demonte to the higher valley of Stura, runs amidst many mountains, which joining one another, and sometimes rising to a very great height, form a part of those alps, by historians and geographers, called maritime alps, separating the valley of Stura and Piedmont, from Dauphiny, and the county of Nice. Towards the middle of the road leading to the top of these mountains, and on the left of the river Stura, we meet with a village called Bergemolo, passing through which village, and still keeping the road through the said valley, we, at about a mile distance, arrive by the way laid down (Plate 1. num. 20.) at a little hamlet called Bergemoletto, containing about one hundred and fifty souls. This hamlet is laid down in the first plate, which exhibits, though not precisely as to distance, the mountains and the houses, part standing and part in ruins, of which we are speaking. From this place

place there run two narrow lanes, both to the right and left, one lefs fteep and fatiguing than the other, and in fome meafure along two vallies, to the mountains number 1. 1. 2. 2. 3. 13. From number 13, which exhibits the flope of the mountain towards the north, to the top of that marked 3; there is no road or path-way whatfoever, and nothing is to be feen on it, but one old, knotty, and almoft branchlefs beech-tree. The fummit of this mountain, as far as number 13, makes with the horizon, an angle much greater than 45°, and fo much greater in fome places, as to be in a manner perpendicular, fo that it is a very difficult matter to climb it, even by a winding path: It is well known that there is no afcending fo fteep a plane, whofe horizontal bafe is lefs than half its height, but by the affiftance of fteps, or at leaft a ferpentine road. The bye lanes on the north fide terminate at number 7, from whence, with fome difficulty, one reaches by a fide road, number 13. In the environs

environs of number 10, and somewhat higher, as well as on the other side, going towards number 8; and near the summits are several copses of beech, birch, and myrtle, whose berries yield food to the pheasants, that often live securely in these mountains; to these copses too, the Alpineers in summer, lead their goats and other cattle to feed in the summer months. From number 12 to number 11, the road is in a manner level; from number 11 to number 10, the steepest ascent of the whole valley, is about a quarter of a mile; and from number 10 to number 9, it is almost three quarters of a mile: I call it the steepest ascent, because, going by the usual path of the Alpineers, from number 10 to number 9, they count about a mile and a half; and from number 11 to number 10, about a mile. On the other side, passing by the valley marked 4 and 8, and going to the summits marked 1, 2. the way is shorter, and the ascent much less disagreeable, for by it one may reach the highest summit of both.

both. At a little distance from Bergemoletto, and on both sides of it to the east and south, we meet with a variety of medicinal and odoriferous plants, such as mountain wormwood, commonly called *Genepi*, gentian, imperatoria, valerian, and veronica; and on the declivity towards the west, there are some meadows which yield tolerable crops of hay, and some corn-fields bearing rye and Indian wheat, the bread of which, with milk and chesnuts, are all the support of the inhabitants. These, however, for the greatest part, though deprived of the numerous conveniences and comforts of life, enjoyed in great towns, and even in the villages of the flat country, live perfectly satisfied with their lot, are strong, hardy, and in general very long lived: as is often the case in mountains, in which we meet with very old men, straight and robust, owing to the wholesomeness of the air and water they enjoy, and the plainness of their diet. About ten years ago, there died in Bergemoletto, one Anthony Bertolotti,

Bertolotti, at the age of one hundred and twelve years, and fometime before, another of one hundred and ten. Now it was from the fummit of the aforefaid mountains marked 1. 1. 2. 2. 3. 13, that fell the valancas of fnow, which did fo much mifchief, and almoft entirely deftroyed the hamlet of Bergemoletto.

According to the obfervations of Kepler, des Cartes, Bartolini, who firft made them in Flanders, and afterwards in the year 1660, in Denmark; likewife thofe of Maffchenbrok, Dortous, Mairan, and others, the fmall particles of which fnow is compofed, are almoft always of a hexagonal form. Des Cartes, indeed, had feen fome that were octangalar, and Bartolini, fome that were pentagonal, and others, fome of various other forms, owing to the union of feveral fmall flakes, in confequence of which, it fometimes refembles wool, and fometimes down, feathers, ftars, wheels, or rofes. But we may eafily conceive, how, by means of its hexagonal figure alone, the

particles

particles of snow can take such hold of each other, as to acquire, when many of them are compressed together, a roundish form. Of this we have an instance, in the snow-balls which children make in winter, by pressing the snow equally on all sides with their hands, as might be done with wax, mud, and such other substances. But this aptness of snow to acquire a roundish form, is most conspicuous in the balls first made by such equal compression and then rolled along the snow; for they so easily lick it up, and so firmly retain it, as to become much larger, and still retain their roundish form; especially if the snow, along which they are thrown, has some declivity, and is so newly fallen, as not to be yet hardened by the frost. Now, by applying what we thus see daily happen in regard to snow-balls to the case in hand, we may easily conceive how a heap of snow, may in its fall, encrease to such a degree, as to form a valanca capable of overwhelming a vast number of houses. The bad weather which prevailed in so many other places,

places, prevailed likewife in the *Forefta* of Bergemoletto. By this word *Forefta*, the Alpineers underftand the villages difperfed over the vallies covered with fmall trees and bufhes, and furrounded with high mountains; for it began to fnow early in March, and the fall encreafed fo much on the 16, 17, 18, and 19, that many of the inhabitants began to apprehend, and not without reafon, that the weight of that which was already fallen, and ftill continued to fall, might crufh their houfes, built with ftones peculiar to the country, cemented by nothing but mud, and a very fmall portion of lime, and covered with thatch laid on a roof of fhingles and large thin ftones, fupported by thick beams. They therefore, got upon their roofs to lighten them of the fnow. At a little diftance from the church marked 7, ftood the houfe of Jofeph Roccia, a man of about fifty, hufband of Mary Anne, born in Demonte, of the family of Bruno; who, with his fon James, a lad of fifteen, had, like his neighbours,

got

got upon the roof of his houfe on the 19th in the morning, in order to leffen the weight on it, and thereby prevent its deftruction. In the mean time, the clergyman who lived in the neighbourhood, and was about leaving home, in order to repair to the church, and gather the people together to hear mafs; perceiving a noife towards the top of the mountains, and turning his trembling eyes towards the quarter from whence he thought it came, difcovered two *Valancas* driving headlong towards the village. Wherefore, raifing his voice, he gave Jofeph notice, inftantly to come down from the roof, to avoid the impending danger; and then immediately retreated himfelf into his own houfe.

Thefe two valancas fet off at once, in a manner, from number 1, 1. 2, 2. and as they ran along a plane forming with the horizon an angle lefs than 45.°, it is pretty evident that they are to be deemed of the firft kind. They met and united at number 8, fo as to form but one valanca; which

which continued to defcend towards the valley, where, on account of the increafe of its bulk, the dimunition of its velocity, and the infenfible declivity of the plane, it ftopped at number 4; and arrefted by the neighbouring mountain, though it covered a large tract of land, did no damage either to the houfes or the inhabitants. Jofeph Roccia, who had formerly obferved that the fall of one valanca, was often attended with that of others, immediately came off the roof at the prieft's notice, and with his fon fled as hard as he could towards the church, without well knowing, however, which way he went; as is ufually the cafe with the Alpineers, when they guefs by the report in the air, that fome valanca is falling, or feeing it fall with their own eyes. The poor man had fcarce advanced forty fteps, when hearing his fon fall juft at his heels, he turned about to affift him, and taking him up, faw the fpot on which his houfe, his ftable, and thofe of fome of his neighbours ftood, converted into

a huge

a huge heap of fnow, without the leaft fign of either walls or roofs. Such was his agony at this fight, and at the thoughts of having loft in an inftant, his wife, his fifter, his family, and all the little he had faved, with many years increafing labour and œconomy, that hale and hearty, as he was, he immediately, as if heaven and earth were come together, loft his fenfes, fwooned away, and tumbled upon the fnow. His fon now helped him, and he came to himfelf little by little; till at laft, by leaning upon him, he found himfelf in a condition to get on the valanca, and in order to re-eftablifh his health there, fet out for the houfe of his friend Spirito Roccia, about one hundred feet diftant from the fpot, where he fell. Mary Anne, his wife, who was ftanding with her fifter-in-law Anne, her daughter Margaret, and her fon Anthony, a little boy two years old, at the door of the ftable, number 15, looking at the people throwing the fnow from off the houfes, and waiting for the ringing of the

bell

bell that was to call them to prayers, was about taking a turn to the houfe, in order to light a fire, and air a fhirt for her hufband, who could not but want that refrefhment after his hard labour. But before fhe could fet out, fhe heard the prieft cry out to them to come down quickly; and raifing her trembling eyes, faw the forefaid valancas fet off, and roll down the fide of the mountain from number 1, 1. 2, 2. and at the fame inftant heard a horrible report from another quarter, which made her retreat back quickly with her family, and fhut the door of the ftable. Happy it was for her, that fhe had time to do fo; this noife being occafioned by another immenfe valanca, the fole caufe of all the mifery and diftrefs fhe had to fuffer for fo long a time. And it was this very valanca, over which Jofeph her hufband was obliged to pafs after his fit, in his way to the houfe of Spirito Roccia.

Some minutes after the fall of the valanca number 1, 1. 2, 2. another huge one broke

broke off from number 3, 13. driing along the valley number 9, 10, 16, 18, 15, 19, 6, 11, 12. it beat down the houfes number 16, 18, 19, 15, 6. which it met in its courfe. This valanca encreafed greatly, by the fnow over which it paffed, in its headlong courfe, and foon reached number 4, 4. with fo much impetuofity, that ftriking againft the firft fallen valanca, it carried away great part of it; then returning back with this reinforcement, it demolifhed the houfes of number 5, ftopping in the valley upon thofe of number 6, 15, 18, which it had already overwhelmed in its firft progrefs: So that, from number 12, 5, 6. to number 18. the fnow lay about forty two of our feet in height, two hundred and feventy in length, and about fixty in breadth. Here it is to be noted, that feven inches and feven lines of our foot of Eliprandus, are equal to the twelve inches of the Paris foot; fo that the height of the fnow, Paris meafure, amounted to more than feventy-feven feet; the length of it to

more

more than four hundred and twenty-seven, and the breadth above ninety-four. Yet this headlong valanca did not all of it reach number 4, some of it having at number 10, struck against the skirt of a mountain, and thereby lost that part, which, considering the direction of its course, would have infallibly demolished the houses of number 11, that remained untouched. Some people affirm, that the concussion of the air occasioned by this valanca, was so great, that it was heard at Bergemolo, and even burst open some doors and windows at that place. This I know, that the damage occasioned by this valanca, was so great, that nothing escaped it in Bergemoletto, but the few houses at number 17, the church number 7, and the house of John Arnaud number 14. The first, by being defended by a rising ground, which separates it from number 5; the church and the house of John Arnaud, by lying out of the direction in which it moved.

The

The inhabitants of Bergemoletto, whom it pleafed God to preferve from this difafter, remained.

" ———— As thofe who from the fhore;
" Joyful and fecure, ftand looking on
" Some wretched fhip, foundering, in the
    " waves,
" And only feel in their breafts that in-
    " nate concern,
" Arifing from a compaffion for the mif-
    " fortunes of others,
" And the fear of what may happen to
    " ourfelves."

Being therefore gathered together, in order to fum up their misfortunes, they firft counted thirty houfes overwhelmed; and then every one calling over thofe he knew, twenty-two fouls were miffing, of which number, was D. Giulio Cæfare Emanuel, their parifh-prieft, who had lived among them forty years. The news of this terrible difafter, foon fpread itfelf over the
            neighbourhood,

neighbourhood, ſtriking all thoſe who heard it, with grief and compaſſion. All the friends and relations of the ſufferers, and many others, flocked of their own accord, from Bergemolo and Demonte; and many were diſpatched by the magiſtrates of theſe places, to try if they could give any relief to ſo many poor creatures, who, perhaps, were already ſuffocated by the vaſt heap of ſnow that lay upon them; ſo that by the day following, the number aſſembled on this melancholy occaſion, amounted to three hundred. Joſeph Roccia, notwithſtanding his great love for his wife and family, and his deſire to recover part of what he had loſt, was in no condition to aſſiſt them for five days, owing to the great fright and grief, occaſioned by ſo ſhocking an event, and the ſwoon which overtook him at the firſt ſight of it. In the mean time, the reſt were trying, if, by driving iron-rods through the hardened ſnow, they could diſcover any roofs; but they tried in vain. The great ſolidity
and

and compactnefs of the valanca, the vaft extent of it in length, breadth and heighth, together with the fnow, that ftill continued to fall in great quantities, eluded all their efforts; fo that after fome days labour, they thought proper to defift from their trials, finding that it was throwing away their time and trouble to no purpofe. The hufband of poor Mary Anne, no fooner recovered his ftrength, than in company with his fon, and Anthony and Jofeph Bruno, his brothers-in-law, who had come to his affiftance from Demonte, where they lived, did all that lay in his power to difcover the fpot, under which his houfe, and the ftable belonging to it, were fituated. But neither himfelf, nor his relations, could make any difcovery capable of affording them the fmalleft ray of comfort; though they worked hard for many days, now in one place, and now in another, unable to give up the thoughts of knowing for certain, whether any of their family was ftill alive, or if they had un-

der

der the snow and the ruins of the stable, found, at once, both death and a grave. But it was all labour lost, so that, at length, he thought proper to return to the house of Spirito Roccia, and there wait, till, the weather growing milder, the melting of the snow should give him an opportunity of paying the last duty to his family, and recovering what little of his substance might have escaped this terrible calamity.

Towards the end of March, the weather, through the lengthening of the days, and the setting in of the warm winds, which continued to blow till about the twentieth of April, began to grow mild and warm; and, of course, the great valanca to fall away partly by exhalation, partly by the action of the winds, which sweep away the more minute particles they meet with on the surface of bodies, and partly by the melting of the snow and ice that composed it; so that little by little, the valley began to assume its pristine form. This change was very sensible, especially

by

by the eighteenth of April, so that the time seemed to be at hand for the surviving inhabitants of Bergemoletto to resume their interrupted labours, with some certainty of recovering a good part of what they had had lost on the unfortunately memorable morning of the nineteenth of March. Accordingly, they dispersed themselves over the valanca, some trying in one place, and some in another, now with long spades, and another time with thick rods of iron, and other instruments proper to break the indurated snow. One of the first houses they discovered by this means, was that of Louisa Roccia, number 16, in which they found her dead body, and that of one of her sons. Next day, in the house called the confreria, number 19, that had two rooms on the ground floor, and one above them, they found the body of D. Giulio Cæsare Emanuel, with his beads in his hand, and two large beams behind him. Joseph Roccia, animated by these discoveries, set himself with new spirits about discovering

covering the fituation of his houfe, and the ftable belonging to it; and with fpades and iron crows, made feveral wide and deep holes in the fnow, throwing great quantities of earth into them; earth mixed with water, being very powerful in deftroying the ftrong cohefion of fnow and ice. On the twenty-fourth, having made himfelf an opening two feet deep into the valanca, he began to find the fnow fofter and lefs difficult to penetrate; wherefore, driving down a long ftick, he had the good fortune of touching the ground with it. We may obferve in the formation of ice, that the firft parts to congeal are thofe on the furface, from whence the congelation extends itfelf, little by little, to the internal parts, till all have loft their motion, and become one folid and compact body: unlefs, indeed, when it happens, that the efficient caufe of the ice, is not ftrong enough to reach a great way, for then the internal parts neareft the earth, remain foft and fluid, while the external ones become hard and

and folid. It is the fame in proportion with fnow, the upper furface of which, is fometimes hard and folid, while that touching the ground, continues lefs compact and refifting. But befides this reafon for the great foftnefs of the lower parts of the valanca, there is another more evident, namely, the heat of the weather, which by infenfibly diffolving the upper fnow, rendered it more apt to penetrate that which lay under it, and fo fit it more eafily to receive the poles thruft into it.

It was no fmall addition to Jofeph's ftrength and fpirit, to be thus able to reach the bottom; fo that he would have joyfully continued his labour, and might perhaps, on that very day, had it not been too far advanced, recovered fome part of what he was looking for, and found that which, affuredly, he by no means expected to meet with. When, therefore, he defifted for that time, it was with much greater reluctance than he had done any of the preceding days. The anxiety of Jofeph, seph, during the following night, may well be compared to that of the weather-beaten mariner, who finding himself, after a long voyage, at the mouth of his desired port, is yet, by the coming on of night, obliged to remain on the inconstant waves till next morning. Those who have experienced what it is to long for a thing at hand, may imagine how often he thought he could discern the rays of the sun peeping over the mountains, in order to resume his labour. Wherefore, at the first gleam of light, he, with his son, hastened back to the spot, where the preceding day he had reached the ground with the stick, and began to work upon it again; but he had not worked long, when lo, to his great surprise, who should he see coming to his assistance, but his two brothers-in-law, Joseph and Anthony Bruno.

Anthony, it seems, the night between the preceding Thursday and Friday, being then in Demonte, dreamed that there appeared to him, with a pale and troubled countenance,

countenance, his fifter Mary Anne Roccia, who, with an earneftnefs intermixed with grief and hope, called upon him for affiftance in the following words : " Anthony, " though you all look upon me as dead in " the ftable where the valanca of fnow " overwhelmed me on the nineteenth of " March, God has kept me alive. Haften " therefore to my affiftance, and to relieve " me from my prefent wretched condi-" tion; in you, my brother, have I placed " all my hopes, dont abandon me; help, " help, I befeech you." Anthony's imagination, was fo affected by the thoughts of thus feeing his fifter, and hearing her utter thefe piteous words, that he immediately ftarted up;

" Like a man who reaffures himfelf in
  " the midft of doubt,
" And changes his fear into comfort,
" Becaufe he has difcovered the truth."

And calling out to his brother Jofeph, he acquainted him with what he had feen and heard.

heard. They both, therefore, as soon as it was day, set out for Bergemoletto, where they arrived a little before eight, tired and out of breath, for they seemed to have their sister continually before their eyes, pressing them for help and assistance. Having therefore taken a little rest and refreshment, they set out again for the place, where Joseph Roccia, and many others, were hard at work in looking for the wrecks of their houses. Joseph had left the spot, where, the day before he thought he had reached the ground, and was trying to reach it in other places. His brothers-in-law immediately fell to work with him, and making many new holes in the snow, the interior parts of which were not so very hard, with the same iron rods, with earth, and with long poles, they at last, about ten, discovered the so long sought for house number 18, but found no dead bodies in it. Knowing that the stable did not lie one hundred feet from the house, they immediately directed their search towards it, and proceed-

ing

ing in the fame manner, about noon, they got a long pole through a hole, from whence iffued a hoarfe and languid voice, which feemed to fay: help, my dear hufband, help, my dear brother, help. The hufband and brother thunderftruck, and at the fame time encouraged by thefe words, fell to their work with redoubled ardour, in order to clear away the fnow, and open a fufficient way for themfelves, to the place from whence the voice came, and which grew more and more diftinct as the work advanced. It was not long, therefore, before they had made a pretty large opening, through which (none minding what danger he expofed himfelf to) Anthony defcended, as into a dark pit, afking who it was, that could be alive in fuch a place. Mary Anne knew him by his voice, and anfwered with a trembling and broken accent, intermixed with tears of joy. " 'Tis I, my dear brother, who am ftill alive in company with my daughter and my fifter-in-law, who are at my elbow.

God, in whom I have always trusted, still hoping that he would inspire you with the thoughts of coming to our assistance, has been graciously pleased to keep us alive." God who had preserved them to this moment, and was willing they should live, inspired Anthony with such strength and spirits, that, notwithstanding the surprize and tenderness, with which so joyful and at the same time so sad a sight must have affected him, had presence of mind enough to acquaint his fellow labourers, all anxiously waiting for the report of his success, that Mary Anne, Margaret, and Anne Roccia were still alive. Whereupon Joseph Roccia, and Joseph Bruno, enlarging the passage as well as they could, immediately followed him into the ruins; whilst the other Alpineers, scattered over the valanca in quest of their lost substance, and the dead bodies of their relations, on the son's calling out to them, flocked round the mouth of the pit, to behold so extraordinary a sight; not a little heightened

tened by that of two live goats fcampering out of the opening. In the mean time, thofe who had defcended into the hole, were contriving how to take out of it the poor and more than half dead prifoners, and convey them to fome place, where they might recover themfelves. The firft thing they did was to raife them up, and take them out of the manger in which they had been fo long ftowed. They then placed them one by one on their fhoulders, and lifted them up to thofe who ftood round the mouth of the pit, who with very great difficulty took hold of them by the arms, and drew them out of their dark habitation. Mary Anne, on being expofed to the open air, and feeing the light, was attacked by a very acute pain in the eyes, which greatly weakened her fight, and was attended with fo violent a fainting fit, that fhe had almoft like to have loft, in the firft moments of her deliverance, that life, which fhe had fo long and with fuch difficulty preferved. But this was a confequence that might be

eafily

eafily forefeen. She had been thirty feven days, fecluded, in a manner entirely, from the open air; nor had the leaft ray of light, in all that time, penetrated her pupils. Such is the action of the folar rays on the eye, that the pupil always adaps itfelf to the quantity of them; opening when the quantity is fmall, and clofing when it is great. It is for this reafon, that going from a very lightfome place, efpecially if we have been in it for fometime, into one much lefs fo, or fomewhat dark, we immediately lofe the capacity of diftinguifhing objects; the pupil being too contracted for the rays of light to enter it in fufficient quantity, fo that we can difcern nothing, until we have been in fuch place long enough for the pupil to return to its primitive configuration. As to the rays of light having fuch a power over our eye, as merely by touching it muft excite in us the fenfation of pain, it is a thing confirmed by numberlefs obfervations. Some perfons cannot

cannot bear walking abroad after a great fall of ſnow, on account of the inſupportable quantity of rays which it throws upon their eyes. Others, who are accuſtomed to ſleep without any light in their chambers, are awakened by the leaſt quantity of light breaking in at the windows. Others, again, who are troubled with inflamations of the eyes, experience the ſharpeſt pains at the admiſſion of the ſmalleſt ray of light. I ſhall ſay nothing of the action of the open air on our bodies, which is, certainly, very great; ſome phiſiologiſts having proved by the exacteſt obſervations, that it is capable of doing the greateſt miſchief to thoſe who have not been expoſed to it for ſome time. Of this I have myſelf had an inſtance in my firſt maſter the late doctor Giovanni Fantoni, a man of great parts and learning, highly eſteemed by foreigners, and father of the plain and only good method of practice, who, after teaching anatomy in our univerſity, of which he was the chief ornament, with the theory and practice of medicine, was promoted to the dignity of reformer and prefident of the faculty. This gentleman on his firft going abroad, after many months confinement by violent contractions of the ftomach, and palpitations of the heart, fuffered fo much from the mere impreffion of the free air, that he was obliged by the moft acute and pungent pains in the head to fhut himfelf up again in his clofet for many months, at the end of which, trying to renew, as he expreffed himfelf, his acquaintance with the open air, he found it was become his enemy to fuch a degree, as to leave him no hopes of being any more able to converfe freely with it. So that after many trials, and at different feafons, he at laft found himfelf obliged to fpend the laft eight years of his life, within the narrow bounds of a fmall bed chamber. If, therefore, the open air can become fo offenfive to thofe, who, though living in places that communicate

with

with it, have not been for some time exposed to its immediate influence, where is the wonder that it should have such influence on a person suddenly brought into it, and who, like Mary Anne had been so long buried forty-two feet deep under the solid snow, as to make her faint away? Her son found means to bring her to herself with a little melted snow, there being nothing else at hand fit for the purpose, and the accident that happened her was improved into a rule for treating the companions of her misfortune. They, therefore, covered all their faces, and wrapped them up so well, as to leave them but just room to breathe, and in this condition took them to number 14, the house of John Arnaud, where Mary Anne was entirely recovered from her fit, by a little generous wine. They then directly placed them in some little beds put up in the stable, which was moderately warm, and almost entirely without light, and prepared for them a mess of rye meal gruel,

mixed

mixed with a little butter; but they could swallow but very little of it, finding their stomachs immediately overloaded, and their respiration, in a manner, taken away by it. The poor creatures had, during the whole time of their confinement, taken but one kind of food, and had, if I may be allowed the expression, given their stomachs so long a holiday, that being now called upon to resume their pristine functions and labours, it was impossible for them not to feel the effects of it. It is the general opinion of the ablest physicians, that none but the slightest food, and this too in small quantities, is fit for those persons who have been obliged by sickness to confine themselves for a long time to a small quantity of nourishment; and the reason of it is evident. In such persons the digestive juices cannot be very active, nor the fibres of the stomach sufficiently strained, so that no solid food, nor even the lightest in large quantities, can be sufficiently penetrated by these juices, nor sufficiently

triturated

triturated by the languid ventricle to yield that mild and sweet liquor, which flowing into the veins, is capable of repairing all the losses of the blood. Hence it is, that when such persons permit themselves to be hurried on by the cravings of too brisk an appetite, or impose upon themselves so far as to think they ought to eat a great deal to recover, and repair their lost strength, in spite of all their physicians can say to them, they soon smart for their folly and intemperance, by pains in the stomach, weakness of the body, and not unfrequently relapses, much more dangerous than the original disorder. The great love and compassion, therefore, of the husband, brothers, and all those about the three poor creatures newly born, as one may say, to the sun, and risen from the dead, made them take on this occasion, all the precautions the weakness of their condition required. The want of food, the moisture and the cold, they had so long suffered, added to their being confined the whole time

time to one posture, had contracted their legs so much, and so greatly weakened their bodies, that they could by no means stand on their feet, and even looked more like dead carcases than living bodies. Their cloaths were almost entirely rotted by the snow water that continually distilled upon them; and Mary Anne's shift in particular was little better than lint, and so impregnated with filth and nastiness, that four washings in boiling lie, were hardly sufficient to make it clean again. It was with great difficulty they could extend their legs, especially the two oldest; and the legs and thighs of Mary Anne were besides swelled greatly. Their friends, therefore, sent the next day for doctor Nicolai of Demonte, to whom I am very much indebted for the full account he gave me of the health of these poor women to the present time; and in the interim, kept them in the stable, which they did not warm a second time, but fed them now and then with the same mess, and with a little

goats

goats milk, to which were added a few spoonfuls of pure wine.

The phyſician, on his arrival the 27th at Arnauld's houſe, found them in the following condition. Mary Anne had a weak and uneven pulſe, complained of a dead pain in the forehead, of frequent ſwimmings of the head, and dimneſs of ſight, and of ſome beginning of ſuffuſion in the eyes, which often ſhed involuntary tears, and the pupil of which was in a conſtant tremulous motion, as it is to this day, of an almoſt inſupportable pain in the ſtomach, of intolerable thirſt, of an unconquerable watchfulneſs, not having had the leaſt ſleep for the laſt eight and forty hours. Her thighs and legs were greatly ſwelled; and, finally, ſhe had almoſt intirely loſt all ſenſe and motion from the region of the loins to the extremities of her feet. The condition of Anne was not quite ſo bad. Her pulſe was leſs languid, and, in a manner, even; but ſhe complained of very

ſharp

sharp pains in the head, very troublesome prickly heat in her feet, attended with such a trembling and weakness, that she could not stand upon them. As to Margaret, all her complaints amounted to no more then a pain in the stomach, and a difficulty of respiration, which, however, did not occasion any disorder in her pulse.

In all very singular accidents, like this under our consideration, it is usual with those who flock about the sufferers, eagerly to enquire from their own mouths the history of their misfortunes, and every minute circumstance that attended it. We may, therefore, imagine, that these poor women must have had many enquiries to answer concerning what happened them while buried under the valanca; such as, what were their first thoughts on finding themselves shut up on every side, what they said to each other, what schemes they formed for their relief, what they lived on, in what posture they lay, what cold they suffered, what sleep they had, and such other

other particulars, as a laudable curiofity might naturally be fuppofed to fuggeft. And, indeed, the phyfician himfelf, who was firft called upon to their relief, found himfelf tempted to afk thefe queftions; but reflecting how improper it was to make them fpeak much in their prefent condition, he not only checked his own curiofity, but that of others, and therefore enjoined them for fome time to a ftrict filence. As to food, he ordered them every three hours, as much veal broth and goats milk their ftomach could bear, with water to extinguifh an intenfe thirft, they continually laboured under. But whatever they put into their mouths, it appeared bitter to them, particularly water, though of different kinds, and from different fprings, and no fuch tafte could be perceived in it by the phyfician or thofe about them. This fenfation of bitternefs lafted in the two eldeft about fifteen days, when it began gradually to wear off, fo as to be entirely gone in a month. To this ordinary diet of

theirs

theirs, was added a spoonful of generous wine twice a day. Margaret was the first to recover her primitive strenght, for eight days after she got out of her bed, she was so strong and hearty, that no one would imagine she had suffered any thing; hence in a few days she returned to her usual kind of life. This was not the case with Anne; for, though she every day grew better and better, it was, notwithstanding, twenty days before she found herself well enough to quit her bed for good and all. These women lived for some time on the diet prescribed by doctor Nicolai, and the dose of wine being encreased in seven days, began to restore them to their appetites. Their next diet consisted of barley gruel boiled without broth, fresh eggs, and a little wheat bread. These precautions answered so well, that Anne was almost entirely recovered by the beginning of June, and in a few days after in a condition to return to her usual country labour. The only thing she still complained of, was a pain

in

in the right knee, which often awakened her in the night, and afflicted her moſt on cloudy and blowing weather. The laſt of all to recover, as I have already ſaid, was the oldeſt Mary Anne. Though the food given them, was of the moiſteſt kind, no ſtools could be obtained from her for fifteen days, whereas Anne had them in two days; and theſe two were very black, and ſo hard, as to be attended with great pains. For the firſt five days ſhe never ſhut her eyes; and the little ſleep ſhe had on the ſixth night, was attended with a difficulty of reſpiration, interrupted by frequent ſtartings, and particularly by frightful dreams, which afflicted her bitterly, ſuch as the tumbling down about her ears, of the ſtable, in which, ſhe, her ſiſter-in-law and her daughter, had been miraculouſly preſerved. Theſe terrors leſſened by degrees, and the twelfth night, for the firſt time, ſhe ſlept ſoundly for four hours, after which ſhe ſeemed to be new born and continued to enjoy that ineſtima-

ble

ble bleſſing. The quantity of her evacuations by urine increaſed proportionally; and in conſequence of it, the ſwelling in her legs and thighs gradually diminiſhed; but as to her ſtomach and eyes, there did not appear in them any great amendment. She could hardly diſtinguiſh any objects and generally ſaw them double; the trembling of the pupil, and the involuntary flow of tears, ſtill continuing; and though this complaint went off, in proportion as ſhe was admitted to a greater quantity of ſolid food and of wine, nevertheleſs it muſt have required a long time; the acute pains returning ſuddenly, as often as ſhe attempted to take of theſe, more than her ſtomach could bear. However, in about ſix weeks, ſhe was able, with ſome difficulty, to get out of bed, and take a few ſteps, ſupported by her huſband and her ſiſter-in-law. This poor woman had ſuffered a great deal more than her daughter, or her ſiſter-in-law, and therefore took a longer time to recover her
ſtrength

strength and spirits. At length, however, at the end of two months, she began to walk about, though still complaining of pains in both her legs, the palpitation in her eyes, and a pain in her stomach, which encreased in proportion as she recovered in other respects, so as to render her utterly unable to return to those country labours, in which before her misfortune, she used to be employed.

These three poor women, with Joseph Roccia, came on the twenty-fourth of July to the baths of Valdieri, to implore the further assistance of our benevolent sovereign, who received them with all that goodness he generally shews to all his subjects, those especially who have met with any misfortunes; and ordered them a new and plentiful supply. The day before they set out from Bergemoletto, which was between eight and nine miles from the baths, and communicates with them by a very tiresome and disagreeable road, passing through the *Foresta* of Valdieri, called the

Desartet

Defartet, where the poor people spent the night in the house of an Alpineer; and the day following arrived at the baths by eight o'clock in the morning. They lay but one night at this place, for on the twenty-fifth they set out again by the same road, stopping at night in the house of the Alpineer, who had entertained them in their way to the baths, and from thence returned to Bergemoletto. I conversed with them the whole day, now with one, and now with another, very minutely concerning their state of health, the life they led before the valanca had shut them up in the ruins of the stable, and all the time they were confined, their conversation in that miserable condition; and, in short, every thing that had happened them to the day they had been dug out.

Mary Anne, when I saw her, which was the twenty-fourth of July, 1755, was about forty years old, very thin visaged, lean, almost entirely bald, troubled from time to time with pains of the head, which
sometimes

sometimes arose in the hind, sometimes in the fore-part, now in one place, and now in another, with protuberances in the feet, and the glands swelled to such a degree, as to retain the hollow made by pressing them with the finger. The pupils of her eyes were greatly dilated, and in a constant tremor; and the eyes of a reddish colour. She could not discover distant objects, thinking she had always before her eyes a thick fog, or impenetrable darkness. She often complained of thirst, and a prickly pain all over her body. She had no sensation of hunger, and being, by my advice, offered a mess of vermicelli broth, in which I had steeped a little bread, she found herself obliged to stop and rest herself a little, after every half dozen spoonfuls, so that it took her a good half hour to eat a porringer of it, which might contain something more than a pound. She eat very little meat, and drank thrice, half a glass of pure wine; saying, that this was the only thing which gave her strength, and

and leſſened the pains of her ſtomach, which returned every time ſhe took any other food. All her animal functions were regular, and two days before the diſcharges peculiar to her ſex had ſtopt in her and her ſiſter-in-law. From the ſecond, of their being buried under the valanca, they had no diſcharges of this kind, till about the twentieth of June, and they returned again the twentieth of July. She generally had from five to ſix hours ſleep every night, but her ſleep was often interrupted by confuſed dreams and ſudden ſtarts. All the foregoing parts of her life, ſhe had enjoyed perfect health, with a very ſharp and quick ſight, free from any trembling of the pupil, or the leaſt diſorder or ſickneſs of any kind. Towards the end of Spring, and during the ſummer and autumn months, ſhe uſed to be conſtantly employed, even from ſun-riſe in the fields, the woods, and the meadows, laying up a ſtock of priviſions for winter, which ſhe ſpent with her huſband in Bergemoletto. About the

age

age of twenty-two, she married Joseph Roccia, and had at six births, three boys and three girls, remaining each time, like the rest of the country women, but very few days within doors, before she returned to her wonted labour. She suckled all her children. She lived upon milk, water, garden-stuff, barley, and sometimes a little wheat bread.

Anne, about twenty-four, of a robust and sanguine constitution, was not so lean or pale-faced. She retained no other signs of all she had suffered in her thirty-seven days burial, but a great thirst, which often tormented her, and that troublesome pain of the right knee, which returned from time to time in cloudy and stormy weather; and after standing a long time, or walking too much. Whatever vegetable food came in her way, she eat it with a good relish and appetite, and drank wine in a middling quantity. By what I have already said of Margaret, a girl of about eleven, the reader may guess that she was

now

now very well, indeed in the best state of health; as, in fact, I saw her, tall and hearty, fat and fresh coloured. She worked, as much as her tender age would permit, in the fields, helping her father, brother, and her aunt, to lay in a stock of provisions for the ensuing winter.

Such was the condition of Mary Anne, Anne, and Margaret Roccia, on the twenty-fourth of July. It is now proper I should say something of the most marvellous circumstance, attending this very singular and surprising accident, I mean their manner of supporting life, during so long and close a confinement. I shall relate what I have heard of it from their own mouths, being the same, in substance, with what count Nicholas de Brandizzo, intendant of the city and province of Cuneo, heard from them on the sixteenth of May, when, by order of our most benevolent sovereign, he repaired to Bergemoletto, effectually to relieve these poor women, and the rest of
the

the inhabitants, who had fuffered by the valanca.

To begin then; on the morning of the twenty-ninth of March, our three poor women, expecting every minute to hear the bell toll for prayers, had in the mean time, taken fhelter from the rigour of the weather, in a ftable built with ftones, fuch as are ufually found in thefe quarters, with a roof compofed of large thin ftones, not unlike flate, laid on a beam ten inches fquare, and covered with a fmall quantity of ftraw, and with a pitch fufficient to carry off the rain, hail or fnow, that might fall upon it. In the fame ftable were fix goats, (four of which I heard nothing of) an afs and fome hens. Adjoining to this ftable, was a little room, in which they had fixed a bed, and ufed to lay up fome provifions, in order to fleep in it in bad weather without being obliged to go for any thing to the dwelling-houfe, which lay about one hundred feet from it. I have already taken notice, that Mary Anne

Anne was looking from the door of the stable at her husband and son, who were clearing the roof of its snow, when warned by a horrible noise, the signal by which the Alpineer knows the tumbling of the valancas, she immediately took herself in, with her sister-in-law, her daughter, and her little boy of two years old, and shut the door, telling them the reason for doing it in such a hurry. Soon after they heard a great part of the roof give way, and some stones fall on the ground, and found themselves involved on all sides with a pitchy darkness; all which they attributed, and with good reason, to the fall of some valanca. Upon this, they for some time thought proper to keep a profound silence, to try if they could hear any noise, and by that means have the comfort of knowing that help was at hand.; but they could hear nothing. They therefore set themselves to grope about the stable, but without being able to meet with any thing but solid snow. Anne light upon the door, and opened it,

hoping

hoping she had found out a way to escape the imminent danger they thought they were in of the buildings tumbling about their ears; but she could not distinguish the least ray of light, nor feel any thing but a hard and impenetrable wall of snow, with which she acquainted her fellow prisoners. They, therefore, immediately began to bawl out with all their might; help, help, we are still alive; repeating it several times; but not hearing any answer, Anne put the door too again. They continued to grope about the stable, and Mary Anne having light upon the manger, it occurred to her, that, as it was full of hay, they might take up their quarters there, and enjoy some repose, till it should please the Almighty to send them assistance. The manger was about twenty inches broad, and lay along a wall, which, by being on one side supported by an arch, was enabled to withstand the shock, and upheld the chief beam of the roof, in such a manner, as to prevent the poor women from being crushed

crushed to pieces by the ruins. Mary Anne placed herself in the manger, putting her son by her, and then advised her daughter and her sister-in-law to do so too. Upon this, the ass which was tied to the manger, frightened by the noise, began to bray and pranse at a great rate; so that, fearing lest he should bring the parapet of the manger, or even the wall itself about their ears; they immediately untied the halter, and turned him adrift. In going from the manger, he stumbled upon a kettle that happened to lie in the middle of the stable, which put Mary Anne upon picking it up, and laying it by her, as it might serve to melt the snow in for their drink, in case they should happen to be confined long enough to want that resource. Anne, approving this thought, got down, and groping on the floor till she had found it, came back to the manger, and put it where her sister-in-law desired her. It seems, the evening before, one of the goats had dropt two dead kids, upon which, Jo-

seph

seph concluded, that she must be greatly out of order, and being desirous (such is the affection of these poor peasants for their cattle, from whom they derive so much profit, and in a manner, their whole subsistence) to relieve the poor creature, had caused a mess of rye porridge to be made for her, and that she might get it the the warmer, had carried it to her in the kettle, in which it had been prepared.

In this situation the good women continued many hours, every moment expecting to be relieved from it; but, at last, being too well convinced, that they had no immediate relief to expect, they began to consider how they might support life, and what provisions they had with them for that purpose. Anne recollected, that the day before she had put some chesnuts into her pocket, but, on counting them, found they amounted only to fifteen. Their chief hopes, therefore, and with great reason now rested on thirty or forty cakes, which two days before had been laid up in the adjoining room. The reader may well imagine, though Anne had never told me a word of it, with what speed and alertness she must, on recollecting these cakes, have got out of the manger, to see and find out the door of the room where they lay; for it is natural with us to be in a great hurry to put in order and make ready, whatever we judge may be wanting to us in any great danger. Accordingly she got out of the manger; but it was to no purpose; she roved and roved about the stable to find out what she wanted, so that she was obliged to come as she went, and take up her seat again amongst her fellow sufferers, who still comforted themselves with the hopes of being speedily delivered from that dark and narrow prison. In the mean while, finding their appetite return, they had recourse to their chesnuts. Margaret and her brother had had their breakfast; so that it was judged they could not suffer much by not eating any more that day; but

Mary

Mary Anne and Anne eat two chefnuts each, and took a little fnow, which they half melted with the heat of their hands. The reft of the chefnuts they referved for a future occafion. They then addreffed themfelves to God, humbly befeeching him to take compaffion of them, and vouchfafe in his great mercy to refcue them from their dark grave, and from the great miferies they muft unavoidably fuffer, in cafe it did not pleafe him to fend them immediate affiftance. They fpent many hours in ejaculations of this kind, and then thinking it muft be night, they endeavoured to compofe themfelves. Margaret and the little boy, whofe tender years prevented their having any idea of what they had to fuffer in their wretched fituation, or any thought of death, and of what they muft fuffer, before they could be relieved, fell quietly afleep. But it was otherwife with Mary Anne and Anne, who could not get the leaft reft, and fpent the whole night in prayer,

prayer, or in speaking of their wretched condition, and comforting one another with the hopes of being speedily delivered from it. As it seemed to them, after many hours, that it was day again, they endeavoured to keep up their spirits with the thoughts, that Joseph with the rest of their friends and relations not getting any intelligence of their situation, would not fail of doing all that lay in their power to come at them. The sensation of hunger was earliest felt by the two youngest; and the little boy crying out for something to eat, and there being nothing for him but the chesnuts, Anne gave him three, and three more to her sister-in-law, and three to her niece, keeping the other four for herself.

I said, that these women seemed to have some notion of the approach of day and night, but I should never have dreamed in what manner this idea could be excited in them, shut up as they were in a body of ice, impervious to the least ray of light,
had

had not they themfelves related it to me. The hens fhut up in the fame prifon, were it feems the clocks, which by their clucking all together, made them think the firft day that it was night, and then again after fome interval that it was day again. This is all the notion they had of day and night for two weeks together; after which, not hearing the hens make any more noife, they no longer knew when it was day or night. I do not remember to have read in any of the writers of natural hiftory, that hens fhut up in a very dark place, where no noife could reach them, cluck at the approach of day and night, or only at indeterminate hours. This I know, indeed, that they have been fometimes obferved in great eclipfes of the fun, to gather together with a great noife, and retire to their roofting places. I know, too, that it is an obfervation of the peafants, that they do the fame in cloudy and dark weather, efpecially during the fummer months, calling upon each other, in their own language,

as

as it were, to avoid the ſtorm. Poulterers, likewiſe, affirm, that when they go, even by night, to catch any chickens in the rooſt, theſe birds awake and cluck at the leaſt noiſe; but that they cluck at theſe ſtated periods, independent of any external ſign, is a thing I have not as yet been able to determine, though with that view I tried the following experiment. I placed eight hens and four pullets, with a ſufficient quantity of food and water, in a very dark place, and to the beſt of my judgment beyond the reach of any noiſe. And then, every morning an hour before day-break, and every evening at night fall, for five days together, I poſted myſelf ſoftly as I could, near the place where they were confined, to hear whether I could diſcover by their clucking any marks of their being able to diſtinguiſh day and night; but with all my diligence and attention, I could never perceive that they made the leaſt noiſe. I muſt own, indeed, that as I had contrived to put them in a place, where

no

no external noife could reach them, their clucking might not have reached me; and fo that the very means I took to make the experiment exactly, might have entirely defeated it. On the other hand, having firft put a peafant in the fame place, and made him imitate the clucking of a hen, I heard the noife he made, though ftanding on the place, from whence I imagined I might have heard the hens themfelves, had they made any. But whatever the inftinct of thefe creatures may be, the three women imagined that the noife of them, was a fufficient fignal to count their days by.

This day the poor women and the boy fupported themfelves with their chefnuts; and at the return of the ufual fignal of night, the boy and Margaret went to fleep; while the mother and aunt fpent it in converfation and prayer. On the next day the afs by his braying, gave now and then, for the laft time, fome figns of life. On the other hand, the poor prifoners had

fomething

something to comfort themselves with; for they discovered two goats making up to the manger, and on feeling them, found one to be a goat in kid, whose time would be up towards the middle of April, the other one of those, which at this time used to supply them with milk. This, therefore, was a joyful event, and they gave the goats some of the hay they sat upon in the manger, shrunk up with their knees to their noses. It then came into Anne's head to try if she could not get some milk from the milch goat; and recollecting, that they used to keep a porringer under the manger for that purpose, she immediately got down to look for it, and happily found it. The goat suffered herself to be milked, and yielded almost enough to fill the cup, which contained above a pint. On this they lived the third day. I could not, on this occasion, but greatly admire the natural simplicity and honest candour of Anne, who being asked, if she, who milked the goat, divided the milk with her fellow-sufferers,

sufferers, and in what manner, made answer. " 'Twas I that milked the goat, and after drinking as much of the milk, as I thought requisite to support nature, I reached the porringer to my sister, who sate next to me, and she after taking some of it, distributed the remainder to her Margaret, and the little boy. I began to take compassion of myself, but without forgetting my companions." The night following the boy and the girl slept as usual, while neither of the two others closed their eyes. Who can imagine how long the time must have appeared to them, and how impatient they must have been to see an end to their sufferings? This, after offering their prayers to the almighty, was the constant subject of their conversation. " O, my husband, Mary Anne used to cry out, if you too are not buried under some of the valancas and dead, why do not you make haste to give me, your sister, and children, that assistance we so much

stand

stand in need of. ? We are thank God, still alive, but cannot hold out much longer, so it will soon be too late to think of us. Ah, my dear brother, added Anne, in you next to God, have we placed all our trust. We are alive, indeed, and it depends upon you to preserve our lives, by digging us out of the snow and the ruins, in which we lie buried." But let us still hope, both of them added, that as God has been pleased to spare our lives, and provide us with the means of prolonging it, he will still in his great mercy put it into the hearts of our friends and relations to use all their endeavours to save us : Yes, they know that we were in the stable, and seeing it covered with snow, they will spare no pains to get at us, and find whether we are dead or alive." To this discourse succeeded new prayers, after which they composed themselves as well as they could, in order to get, if possible, a little sleep.

The

The hens having given the usual signal of the return of day, they began again to think on the means of spinning out their lives. Mary Anne bethought herself anew of the cakes put up in the adjacent room; and upon which, could they but get at them, they might subsist a great while without any other nourishment. On the first day of their confinement, they had found in the manger a pitch fork, which they knew used to be employed in cleaning out the stable, and drawing down hay through a large hole in the hay-loft, which lay over the vault. Anne observed, that such an instrument might be of service in breaking the snow, and getting at the cakes, could they but recover the door leading into the little room. She, therefore, immediately got out of the manger, from which she had not stirred since the first day; and groping about, sometimes meeting with nothing but snow, sometimes with the wall, and sometimes loose stones, she, at length, light upon a door, which

she

she took for the stable door, and endeavoured to open it as she had done the first day, but without success; an evident sign that the superincumbent snow had acquired a greater degree of density, and pressed more forcibly against it. She, therefore, made step by step, the best of her way back to the manger, all the time conversing with her fellow sufferers; and taking the fork with her, continued to rove and grope about, till at last she light upon a smooth and broad piece of wood, which to the touch had so much the appearance of the little door, as to make her hope she had at last found what she had been so earnestly looking for. She then endeavoured to open it with her hands, but finding it impossible, told the rest that she had a mind to employ the pitch fork; but Mary Anne dissuaded her from doing so. " Let us,
" said she, leave the cakes where they are
" a little longer, and not endanger our
" lives any further, by endeavouring to
" preserve them. Who knows but with
" the

"the fork, you might make such destruc-
"tion, as to bring down upon our heads,
"that part of the stable that still continues
"together, and which, in its fall, could
"not fail of crushing us to pieces. No,
"God keep us from that misfortune.
"Lay down your fork Anne, and come
"back to us, submitting yourself to the
"holy will of the Almighty, and patiently
"accept at his hands whatever he may
"please to send us." Anne, moved by such
sound and affecting arguments and reasons,
immediately let the fork fall out of her
hands, and returned to the manger. "Let
"us, continued Mary Anne, let us make
"as much as we can of our nursing goats,
"and endeavour to keep them alive by
"supplying them with hay. Here is a
"good deal in the manger, and it occurs
"to me, that when that is gone, we may
"supply them from another quarter, for
"by putting up my hand, trying what
"was above me, I have discovered that
"there is hay in the loft, and that the hole
"to

" to it is open, and juft over our heads;
" fo that we have nothing to do, but to
" pull it down for the goats, whofe milk
" we may fubfift upon, till it fhall pleafe
" God to difpofe otherwife of us."

This reafoning, was not only found in itfelf, but fupported by facts; for ever since their confinement, they had heard ftones fall from time to time upon the ground, and thefe ftones could be no others than thofe of the building, which the fhock of the valanca had firft loofened, and which the weight it every day acquired by encreafing in denfity, afterwards enabled it to difplace. Wherefore, had fhe happened to difturb with the pitch-fork, as there was the greateft reafon to fear fhe might, any of thofe parts, which, united together, ferved to keep up the beam that fupported the great body of fnow, under which they lay buried, the fall of the ftable, and their own deftruction, muft have infallibly been the confequence of it. I do not deny but that this beam was ftrong enough to bear a much

greater

greater weight. For, suppofing its prefent pofition in the ftable, the fame with that in which it was afterwards found, and which I shall prefently defcribe, the cavity formed by it was fix feet long, and two feet and a half high at one end, the length therefore of that part of the beam, which lay over this cavity, was about ten feet and a half. Furthermore, fuppofing that this cavity was four feet broad, the roof fupported by this beam muft have meafured fix and twenty fuperficial feet, which multiplied by forty two feet, the height of the valanca, give one thoufand and ninety-two cubit feet for the quantity of fnow fupported by the roof. By experiments made to afcertain the quantity of air, that flies off in the melting of fnow, which experiments I fhall prefently relate; it appears that the volume of fnow compreffed, and ftrongly fqueezed into a veffel, is to the volume of the fame fnow reduced to water, as feventeen to fix ; wherefore, fuppofing the fnow upon the roof to have

been

been more condenfed to a much greater degree, we may allow that the volume of it, in this its folid form, was to its volume when melted, as two to one; fo that the one thoufand and ninety-two feet of folid fnow, muft yield five hundred and forty-fix cubic feet of melted fnow. Now, a cubic foot of water, weighs about three hundred and twelve pounds, therefore the weight of the fnow fupported by the roof, amounted to no lefs than one hundred and feventy thoufand, three hundred and fifty-two pounds. By obfervations made on the ftrength of timber, it appears that a beam of larch, clean and free from knots, and every other imperfection, efpecially at or near the middle, eleven inches fquare, and fix feet and a half long, can bear, if placed horizontally on its two extremities, a weight of two hundred thoufand pounds, fufpended to the middle of it; and that it can bear a ftill greater weight in an oblique pofition. It therefore follows, that as in the prefent cafe, the beam did not lie horizontally,

zontally, and had befides the weight of the fnow difpofed over its whole length, and not confined to its middle, it could not but eafily bear it; fince there wanted twenty-nine thoufand fix hundred and forty-eight pounds of the total weight which it might have fupported, even in the moft difadvantageous pofition and circumftances. But after all, had the parts which kept up the beam, been removed, it muft then, with all the great weight upon it, have tumbled into the ftable, to the unavoidable deftruction of the poor people confined in it.

This day the fenfation of hunger was more and more lively and troublefome, without their having any thing to allay it with but fnow, and the milk yielded them by one of the goats their fellow prifoners. I fay one of the goats, for as yet they had milked but one of them, thinking it would be ufelefs, or rather hurtful, even if they could, to take any milk from that in kid. Anne had recourfe to the other, and in the whole day, got from her about two pounds of milk, on which, with the addition of a little snow, picked up in the corner between the beam and the floor, they subsisted. This day, too, they began to be troubled with a great dryness in their mouths, and a violent thirst, which they endeavoured to allay, by often putting snow into their mouths. It was the last day of Mary Anne's having all the benefits of nature in a regular course, having for the following thirty-three days, had no sensible evacuation but that of urine, which the two others likewise continued always to have, with this difference, that Anne had but two stools the whole time, whereas Margaret had one every five or six days. Anne, Margaret, and the little boy, slept the next and all the following nights; but as to Mary Anne, she passed it as she had done the preceding nights; nor did she ever, during the thirty-seven days of her confinement, close her eyes, and take any sleep, except three times, and that, as well as she could guess, for about two hours each time.

The

The poor creatures spent the fifth day in the same manner. The sixth was attended with a new source of affliction and distress.

The little boy Antony, who subsisted entirely on milk, not being able to bear the cold of the snow in his mouth, began on this day to complain of very cruel pains in his stomach and belly, which made him work and writh a thousand and a thousand ways without finding the least ease or relief. The poor mother endeavoured to warm and cheer up the poor creature, by closing him to her bosom, the only way left her to do it. This gave him some ease, but he had but just strength enough to taste a little milk which was put to his lips. A good many hours after this, his pains returned, when his mother and his aunt, taking him by turns, on their laps, and closing him to their bosoms, did all their own wretched condition and situation would let them, to give him ease and quiet him. In this condition, the poor little creature lingered on in incredible pains, to the unspeakable affliction

fliction of the poor women, who had forgot their own sufferings to attend entirely to his. On the tenth day of his illness, reckoning the days by their usual clock, viz. one of the hens that still survived, he was so very bad, as no longer to bear lying in his mother's or his aunt's lap; and therefore desired to be stretched at length in the manger. This the tender mother complied with, and with much difficulty laid him alongside herself, her great affection for him not permitting her, as long as she could herself afford him any assistance, to part with him to his aunt or his sister. In this situation, he did nothing but complain, his weak and piteous cries piercing deeper and deeper into the heart of the poor mother, who, though it was with the utmost difficulty she could turn about in her confined situation, never ceased either warming his feet or mouth with her breath, or by stroking him with her hands, endeavouring to find out whether he was dead or alive. At length, after he he had lain quiet for a little time, she all at once found her fingers seized and squeezed by the death-cold hands of the poor innocent; which she considered an evident sign of his being near his end. She therefore took him up in the best manner she could, laid him in her lap, and by stroaking with her hands, his already benummed legs and thighs, now too weak to support his little emaciated body, and giving a thousand kisses, and breathing frequently on his cold lips, in order to impart some heat to them, at last brought him to give a faint sigh, on which dipping her trembling fingers into the milk, she let a few drops of it fall into his mouth. Upon this, the poor creature cried out with another sigh, " O my father, my father! and " he, too, is under the snow, O my fa-" ther, my father!" These words were scarce out of his mouth, when the mother felt his head falling back upon her arm. The grief and affliction which the poor mother felt at this moment, the last for certain of her child's life, and the deep impression made on her heart by his last words, " O my father, my father, he, too, is " under the snow; O my father, my fa-" ther!" made her burst out into a flood of tears, which from her cheeks trickled down on the face of her dead child, whom with repeated kisses, she fain would have brought to life again. At length, his face being grown quite cold, and no motion remaining in his arms or legs, which when lifted up, fell back by their own weight, she cried out to her sister-in-law. " Ah, sister, he is now dead indeed, my " boy is dead, who remembered his fa-" ther with his last breath. I have often " before heard the poor creature speak of " his father, who indeed, is perhaps bu-" ried under the snow, and no longer in " the land of the living, as we are, through " the special mercy of the Lord, and now " he has mentioned him again with his " last breath. Who knows what will be-" come of us, who have suffered so much,

and

" and so long, by cold, by hunger, and
" by want of sleep, in this dark dungeon?
" He, as more delicate and less inured
" to sufferings is gone first, who knows
" which of us is next to follow him? O
" my dear child, have I lost you at last."
The sister, though sorely afflicted at the loss of her nephew, and touched by these words of Mary Anne; nevertheless, to lessen in some manner, her extreme agony, took from her the dead body of the child, and after first stripping it of its cloaths, laid it in the furthest corner of her end of the manger.

The death of this poor child, proved the severest trial that the three women, the two eldest especially, had to suffer during their long confinement; and from this unfortunate day, the fear of death, which they considered as at no great distance, began to haunt them more and more. Nor is it, I believe, any hard matter to conceive that this must have been the case, considering that we are more moved by those

events

events which nearly concern us, and we fee happen to perfons in the fame fituation with ourfelves, than by thofe, which we only think of as poffible; and therefore may flatter ourfelves with the hopes of being able to efcape. The little nourifhment, which the goat yielded the poor women, had made them fuffer greatly on the preceding days; they were, befides, benumbed, or rather frozen with the intenfe cold. Add to this, the neceffary, but inconvenient and tormenting pofture of their feet, knees, and every other part of their bodies; the fnow, which melting over their heads, perpetually trickled down their backs, fo that their clothes, and their whole bodies were perfectly drenched with it: the ftench arifing from the dead bodies, and their own, and the goats excrements, were fuch, that they were often on the point of fwooning away with it, and obliged to keep themfelves from fainting, by handling the fnow, and putting fome of it into their mouths: the thirft with which

their

their mouths were conſtantly burnt up; the thoughts, that in all this time no one had been at the pains to look for and relieve them; the conſideration that, all they had hitherto ſuffered, was nothing in compariſon of what they had ſtill to ſuffer before they could recover their liberty, or ſink under the weight of all the evils which encompaſſed them; all theſe, certainly, were circumſtances ſufficient to render them to the laſt degree, wretched and miſerable. But after all, the ſight of death, till this day, was but a pretty diſtant proſpect; for though it was preſent to their thoughts, yet, as they did not behold it with their own eyes, they flattered themſelves that they might one way or another, eſcape it. But now that they ſaw it come down among them, it was impoſſible that they ſhould not be to the laſt degree afflicted and terrified at ſuch ſhocking company. Add to this, that the milk of their fond and loving nurſe, fell away little by little, till at length, inſtead of about two pounds,

pounds, which she, in the beginning, used to yield, they could not now get so much as a pound from her. The hay that lay in the manger was all out, and it was but little the poor women could draw out of the hole which lay above them; so that as the goats had but little fodder, little sustenance could be expected from that which they thought proper to milk. These animals were become so tame and familiar, in consequence of the fondness shewn them, that they always came on the first call to the person that was to milk them, affectionately licking her face and hands. Anne, encouraged by this tameness of theirs, bethought herself of accustoming them to leap upon the manger, and from thence upon her shoulders, so as to reach the hole of the hay-loft, and feed themselves; so apt is hard necessity to inspire strength and ingenuity. She began by the goat that yielded them milk, helping her up into the manger, and then putting her upon her shoulders. This had the desired effect, the animal being

ing thereby enabled to reach much farther with its head, than they could with their hands. They did then the fame by the other goat, from whom, as foon as fhe fhould drop her kid, they expected new relief; fhe too, in the fame manner, found means to get at the hay, which afforded the poor women fome relief in the midft of their prefling neceffity. After this day, the goats required no further affiftance, they fo foon learned to leap of themfelves on the manger, and from thence on the womens fhoulders. But we muft not conclude that hunger was the chief of the poor womens fufferings; far from it. After the firft days, during which it proved a fore torment to them, they, through neceffity, grew fo accuftomed to very little, and very light nourifhment, that they no longer felt any fenfation of that kind, but lived contentedly on the fmall quantity of milk they could get from their goat, mixed with a little fnow. Their breath was what gave them moft uneafinefs; for it began to be very difficult on the fifth or sixth day, every inspiration being attended with the sensation of a very heavy and almost insupportable load upon their chests. Besides this, the ice-cold water, which was constantly dropping on their bodies, and the continual bitings of the lice, with which, they were, in a manner, eaten up, proved a perpetual source of uneasiness and torment to them. This last plague there was no getting rid of, and therefore they were obliged to make a virtue of necessity, and patiently submit to it. As to the constant dripping, with which they were almost frozen to death, they endeavoured to guard against it; Margaret, by putting the kettle on her head; and her mother and aunt, by wrapping themselves up in the things of which Anne had stript the little boy's body, especially about the head, as the part which stood most in need of defence. This covering afforded the two eldest some relief, but it was of short duration; for the cloaths, when saturated with water, proved

a heavy

a heavy burthen, and a much greater evil than what they endeavoured to shun by using them, so that they were at last forced to throw them off, and submit entirely to God's providence. Anne was for having the kettle serve as an umbrella to all the three; and with this view, put a little of it over her head; but the affectionate mother, having her daughter's welfare more at heart than her own, left her share to the girl, and found means to make the aunt follow her example; so that not a word more passed upon this article.

They now had lost all means of guessing at the returns of day and night; and their only employment was to recommend themselves fervently to God, beseeching him to take compassion of them, and at length, put an end to their miseries, which encreased from day to day. At last; their nurse growing dry, they found themselves without any milk, and obliged to live upon snow alone for two or three days, Mary Anne not approving an expedient proposed by by her sister. This was to endeavour to find out the carcasses of the hens; for as they had not heard them for some days past, they had sufficient reason to think they were dead; and then eat them, as the only thing with which they could prolong life. But Mary Anne, rightly judging that it would be almost impossible to strip them clean of their feathers, and that besides, the flesh might be so far putrefied, as to do them more harm than good, thought proper to dissuade her sister from having recourse to this expedient, at least for the present. " Let us endeavour, said she, " since we have already suffered so much, " to put up with the snow, and try if we " cannot, by means of it, hold out a little " longer, and keep body and soul toge- " ther." But the unspeakable providence of God, whose will it was they should live, provided them with new means of subsistence, when least they expected it, by the kiddening of the other goat. They had often thought of this, and consulted

together

together what they should do if they should then happen to be alive. They resolved, in order to prevent the kid's robbing them of any milk, to kill it the minute it was dropt, and perhaps divide it amongst themselves and eat it, in case they have nothing else left to live upon. The cries and throws of the goat at length giving notice, that she was about to drop her burthen, they called her to them, and found it to be really the case. Anne, therefore, helped the poor thing into the manger, and, delivering her of a kid, gave it to the sister, who immediately killed it. She then got the dam to leap upon her shoulders, and feed herself. By this event, they judged themselves to be about the middle of April; wherefore, after offering God their most humble thanks, for having preserved them so long, in the midst of so many, and such great difficulties, they again beseeched him to assist them effectually, till they could find an opportunity of escaping their doleful prison, and

see

see an end to their great sufferings. Their hopes of this their humble supplication being heard, were raised on the appearance of this new supply, and on their reflecting that the snow begins to thaw in April; in consequence of which, either that about the stable would soon dissolve enough to let some ray of light break in upon them, or at least put their relations upon endeavouring to get at their bodies, in order to bury them. Mary Anne told me, that, though she was thoroughly sensible of the badness of her condition, in which it was impossible for her to hold out much longer, and saw it every day grow worse and worse; she never, however, despaired of her living to be delivered from it. She thought she continually heard within her, a voice saying, " God will send you assistance ; your " husband has not forgot you, and is in- " tent upon recovering you; your bro- " thers in Demonte will never rest till they " know with certainty whether you are " dead or alive." Now and then, however,
whilst

whilst her sister and daughter were asleep, she used to weep bitterly; one time thinking of the little appearance there was of her ever escaping, and that her husband and the boy that was at work with him, were themselves buried under the valanca, and dead; another time, reflecting on the death of her little boy, a presage, as it were, to herself and her fellow sufferers, of what they themselves had to expect; now on her heavy sins, in which the Lord might think proper to call her away. And she sometimes suffered herself to be so overcome by these reflections, that she more than once feared her sighs and sobs would suffocate her. They once awakened Anne, who asking her the cause of this her new grief, received for answer, that her tears were owing to her sufferings, with which she was already beyond measure afflicted, and yet increased from day to day, whilst her strength to bear them, continually diminished. " God, replied the sister, who
" has assisted us all this time, will not de-
" sert

"sert us at present; let us patiently wait "his pleasure with regard to us, and con-"tinue to trust in him our only refuge. "He has rescued us from death, which "would certainly have been our lot, had "the stable been entirely demolished. He "has not altogether deprived us of subsis-"tence, having left us two goats, from "whom, little as it is, we have obtained "some nourishment. He, notwithstand-"ing the cold, with which we are almost "frozen to ice; notwithstanding the wa-"ter with which we are almost drowned; "notwithstanding all the other evils with "which we are surrounded, is graciously "pleased to grant us life; therefore let us "not grow weary of beseeching him, ef-"fectually to hear our prayers, and deli-"ver us from this dark grave." These, with other words full of hope and confi-dence, gave much comfort to Mary Anne, so that she replied with a sigh: "You are "in the right, sister, let us pray God not to "grow weary of protecting us, and beseech
"him

"him to infpire, at leaft my brothers,
"to haften to our affiftance; from them I
"firmly truft in God to obtain it; for
"they were not within the reach of the
"valanca, which has overwhelmed us,
"and perhaps your brother and my fon
"Anthony, and Jofeph Bruno, are, if it
"fhall fo pleafe God, to be our deli-
"verers. I know how much they love
"me, and what great lengths they would
"go to affift me." With this, and fuch
like pious difcourfe, the poor women endeavoured to comfort themfelves, and to
keep up their fpirits, in patient expectation
of the happy moment they fo much long-
ed for. For my part, I cannot fufficiently
admire the courage and intrepidity of
Anne, who told me, that in all this time,
fhe never let a tear efcape her but once.
This was on its occurring to her, that, as
they muft at length perifh for want, it might
fall to her lot to die laft. For the thought
of finding herfelf amidft the dead bodies of
her fifter and her niece, herfelf too in a
dying

dying condition, terrified and afflicted her to such a degree, that she could no longer command her tears; but wept bitterly.

I observed, that the goat had kidded. This event afforded the poor women a new supply of milk, Anne for a while getting two porringers at a time from her, with which they recruited themselves a little. But as the goats began to fall short of hay, the milk of the only one that gave them any, began to lessen in proportion, so that at length they saw themselves reduced to a single, and even half a porringer. It was, therefore, happy for them, that the time drew nigh, in which God had purposed to rescue them from their horrible prison and confinement, and put an end to their sufferings. One time they thought they could hear a noise of some continuance at no great distance from them. This was probably the 20th, when the parish priest's body was found in the house number 19. And, upon it, they all together raised their weak and

hoarse

hoarse voices, crying out, " Help, help :" but the noise ceased, and they this time neither saw or heard any thing else that might serve as a token of their deliverance being at hand. However, this noise alone was sufficient to make them address God with greater fervour than ever, beseeching him to have compassion on them, and to confirm them still more and more in their warm hopes, that the end of their long misery was not far off. In fact, they again heard another noise, and that nearer them, as though something had fallen to the ground. On this they again raised their voices, and again cried out: " Help, " help :" but no one answered, and soon after the noise itself entirely ceased. Their opinion concerning this noise, and in this they certainly were not mistaken, was that it came from the people, who were at work to find them, and who left off at the approach of night, and went home with a design to return to their labour the next morning. After the noise of the body

fallen

fallen to the ground in their neighbourhood, they seemed for the first time to perceive some glimpse of light. The appearance of it scared Anne and Margaret to the last degree, as they took it for a sure fore-runner of death, thought it was occasioned by the dead bodies; for it is a common opinion with the peasants, that those wandering wild-fires, which one frequently sees in the open country, are a sure presage of death to the persons constantly attended by them, which ever way they turn themselves; and they accordingly call them death-fires. But Mary Anne, was very far from giving into so silly a notion. On the contrary the light inspired her with new courage, and she did all that lay in her power to dissipate the fears of her sister and daughter, revive their hopes in God, and persuade them that their deliverance and the end of all their sufferings was at hand; insisting that, this light could be no other than the light of heaven, which had, at least, reached

the

the stable, in consequence of the valanca's melting, and still more in consequence of the constant boring and digging into it, by their relations in order to come at their dead bodies. " Let us, continued she, " my dear Anne and Margaret, let us " with redoubled fervour and joy thank " God, and humbly beseech him to con-" tinue his protection to us, that we may " at last get alive out of this dungeon, in " which he has so miraculously preserved " us. Let us thank him for his great " mercy towards us, and beseech him not " to desert us in these last moments. Let " us trust in his promises, who says, I will " not forsake you, I will not abandon you. " To-morrow morning we shall again hear " them at work, and be convinced, that the " light we now see is the light of heaven, which " has, at last, found its way to our longing " eyes." Mary Anne guessed right what was to happen the next day, for it was the next day that Anthony descended into the ruins of the stable, and to his unspeakable

surprise

surprise found the poor women alive blessing and exalting the most high, and restored them from darkness to light, from danger to security, from death to life, by drawing them out of the manger, and removing them to the house of Joseph Arnaud; where they continued to the end of July, living in the manner I have already related.

Thirty-seven entire days did these poor women live in the most horrible sufferings occasioned no less by filth and the disagreeable posture they were confined to, than by cold and hunger; but the Lord was with them. He kept them alive, and they are still living, in a new cottage built the same year in the *Foresta* of Bergemoletto, at no great distance from their former habitation. I shall relate in what manner they have lived since, and in what state of health they now are. But shall first endeavour to account for their holding out so long in such terrible circumstances, the singularity of which has been matter of much

much inveftigation with all thofe, who have heard of this furprifing event, and is apt to excite that laudable curiofity, which fo much tends to the improvement of the fciences: for it appears at firft fight, that, the exceffive cold they themfelves own they fuffered, or their almoft total want of food, or the badnefs of the air, which on account of the narrow bounds of their prifon, they muft have breathed again and again, until it had loft all power of expanding and working their lungs; it appears I fay, at firft fight, that any of thefe circumftances fhould, alone, have been fufficient to put a fpeedy end to their lives. It is true, indeed, that their continuing fo long in a place but twenty inches broad, with their backs to the wall, their toes under their hams, and their knees to their nofes, occafioned in the two oldeft fuch violent complaints in the feet, that they have not as yet got the better of them: it is true, likewife, that their ftomachs, through the fmallnefs and lightnefs of their food, have fuffered
excef-

excessively; in short, it is true, that the eyes of Mary Anne were rendered tremulous by the first rays of the sun, that re-entered them, and that she is losing her sight little by little: all this, no doubt, is very true; but it is likewise very true, that they were in the circumstances already described, and continued in it a long while, and yet are still alive: an event the like of which, as I observed at setting out, I do not remember to have ever heard or read of.

Scheuchzer relates, that in the country of Glaris, a boy driving home some cows, was overtaken and rolled up along with them by a valanca, which likewise covered a spring at which he happened to be watering them, and the field in which it lay. His relations lost no time in trying for him by boring the snow with long poles, now in one place and now in another; but they could meet nothing like him the first day. The next day some neighbours, whom they had invited to their assistance,

in

in turning over the snow, in order to find '˚s dead body and bury it, to their very great surprise found him alive. A girl of fourteen, buried by another valanca in company with thirteen persons, was dug out alive at the end of three days; but then she was the only person that had the good fortune to escape. Six and twenty persons were buried by a valanca at saint Theodore's; and Pietro Gulero, a man of eighty-five, was dug alive out of it at the end of three days. I omit other accounts given by Scheuchzer of persons drawn alive out of valancas, after lying in them a few hours; knowing that such things sometimes happen in our own mountains, in which, towards Limone, as I have been told by a person of credit, a priest and two peasants were in 1747, dug alive out of a valanca, in which they had lain three days. But I see no difficulty in accounting for all this; nothing more being requisite, than that the snow should be loose and soft enough to let the unhappy

prisoners

prisoners make an opening to breathe by from their mouths to the open air. And, in fact, this is nearly the way, which the Laplanders, according to Scheffer, take in the open country to avoid being stifled by the great quantities of snow, that the westerly winds often carry with them. " Unum genus est," writes Scheffer speaking of these winds, " uti testati sunt mihi " qui viderunt, surgens a mari, quod cum spirare incipit, densas, crassasque media æstate, dieque creat nebulas, quibus longior omnibus prospectus intercipitur. Hyberno autem tempore tantam nivium dejicit vim, atque copiam, ut si quem deprehendat in campis, illi non aliud supersit remedium, quam ut projectus in terram, veste se operiat, obruique sinat nivibus, donec tempestas desierit." The difference is, that in all the accidents I have been just relating, the time, those dug alive out of the snow had remained in it, was almost nothing to the thirty-seven days, which the poor women had
been

in queſtion had been buried in it. The fame thing may be faid, if we confider the fmallnefs and lightnefs of their food during that very long period.

We have a great many accounts of people, who have lived for a long time without any kind of nouriſhment; but of thefe accounts, as fome are true, fo fome are entirely falfe; and others partly true and partly falfe. Pechlin's little work, "De aeris, et alimenti defectu, et vitâ fub aquis," has the following words in the beginning of the twelfth chapter. " Tot virorum eruditorum teftimoniis, argumentifque probata eft abftinentium hiftoria, ut qui illam inficiari aufus fit, etiam meridiani folis lucem negare videri velit. Ego quidem, ut non improbo inediæ quædam portenta, fic non temere omnibus accedo; multa enim profecto funt fabulofa, aliqua intra famam, plurima non nifi, certis circumftantiis vera, alias falfa deprehenfa." And certainly it is the part of a prudent and circumfpect man not to fwallow too readily what some people relate, merely with a view to surprise and astonish; but, on the other hand, it is equally his duty not to deny a thing stiffly, because he does not comprehend it at first sight: just as a man of sense will neither decide peremptorily concerning things, for and against which, the proofs are equally probable; nor, on the other hand, speak doubtfully of those which are clear and evident; since to act in this manner, is to fight against truth, and to the utmost of our power stifle it. Now we need only give a look into Fernelius, Citesius, Licetus, Lentulus, the *Journal des Sçavans*, the Memoirs of the Royal Academy of Sciences at Paris, the Essays and Observations of the Edinburgh Society, Vandermonde's Medicinal Journal, and other books, to meet with many histories of this kind. In one of them, we read of a young woman, who, on falling out of a coach, and being trampled on the head by a horse, and run over the back near the eleventh vertebra, by a wheel,

wheel, was immediately seized with a vomiting of blood, which was followed by a high fever, accompanied with dangerous symptoms, and such a constriction of the fauces, as for two years together, prevented her from swallowing more than a few crumbs of bread, two glasses of water, and a little syrup every twenty-four hours. In another place, we meet with another girl, who lived without any nourishment, liquid or solid, for three years. This girl was at first seized with a fever and a vomiting; then she lost her speech, and became paralytical all the body over, except the head, in which the fauces alone were effected, and took an aversion to every kind of food. At the end of six months, she recovered the use of her limbs, but her aversion to food continued, nor had she any evacuation during the whole time. Her skin, indeed, retained its smoothness, but grew cold to such a degree, that no rubbing or friction could bring any heat into it. We read of a third, who having little by little,

lost

lost all sensation of hunger and thirst, became at length so patient of abstinence, that for some months together she took no sustenance. The news of which being spread abroad, she was by orders of the supreme magistrates of Berne, removed to the hospital, and narrowly watched both by the physicians and those about her; who all affirmed, that she really eat nothing; for which reason she was carried home again, where she continued to live many years in the same manner.

We shall also find that an inhabitant of Cologne, seized with a melancholy madness, lived seven weeks on a little water every day, or every second day; and that an inhabitant of Harlaem, seized with a raving madness, lived forty days on nothing but the smoke of tobacco, now and then rinsing his mouth with water; that a pregnant woman, the superior orifice of whose stomach was so closely shut up, that no food, solid or liquid, could pass it, lived two ... together without eating or drinking
any

any thing; that a girl through some family pique, passed eighteen days without eating or drinking, except that on the sixteenth day, she took a little cake steeped in water. All France had heard of the abstinence of father Leaulté, a Benedictine monk, who for upwards of twenty years, celebrated mass every day during the whole lent, and took no kind of nourishment. And all Italy has heard of a Jewish woman called Ricca, who, seized with extraordinary symptoms, which took their rise from a suppression of the menses, and from a great lowness of spirits, passed upwards of seven months without retaining on her stomach either food or physic; nay, all endeavours to nourish her with clysters made of chicken or capon broth, proved ineffectual, as she could not take them in, or, when she did, could not keep them. Some travellers assure us, that not a few of the inhabitants of the Canadian forests, pass long intervals without any kind of solid food, contenting themselves with water and the fumes

fumes of tobacco; and that a great number of catholicks, shut up in the prisons of Cochinchina, being refused any food, lived without it many months. I omit what Plato says in his tenth dialogue on the republic. " Verily, I shall not tell you a
" story of Erus, an Armenian, a brave
" man of the Pamphilian family, who
" having some time ago fallen in battle,
" was ten days after, when they were ta-
" king away the other, now putrefied bo-
" dies, found without any signs of putre-
" faction; and being brought home to
" receive the last offices, came to himself
" the twelfth day, after they had placed
" him on the funeral pile." Nor of the seven famous sleepers in the time of Valentinian; nor of what is reported of Empedocles, that he used to make men live thirty days together without eating or drinking; nor of the Lucomori of Russia, who sleep the whole winter shut up in their houses, till the return of spring, when they get up, and again make their appearance, for these

are

are considered as fabulous relations, by the most inquisitive writers; and, besides, I imagine, that the few I have above cited, are sufficient to prove, that men can live for some time at least, without food; and for a still much longer time on very little. For these, were there no other instances, whereas there are almost without number, would alone be sufficient to establish the possibility of what I myself have related concerning the women confined in the stable overwhelmed by the valanca; whose long abstinence, however, compared with that of others, we shall find much more extraordinary on account of certain circumstances that attended it. Most of those persons, whom we know to have lived without food, were reduced to that condition by disorders, which prevented any food from getting into the stomach; or else the animal functions in them were so much obstructed, as to put a stop to digestion, chylification, and every other of those separations and excretions, from whence proceeds the neceffity of new nourifhment. Whereas thefe three poor women were, at the time this misfortune happened them, in the beft ftate of health, and all their lives accuftomed to hearty living like all other country folks, fo that it was neceffity alone, that hindered them from allowing their bodies the fupport they required; it being evident, that their abftinence from food, was not owing to want of excretion, but the much felt want of food. But we fhall fee prefently, that it is not in this light alone, their cafe is fo fingular. What really renders it fingular to the laft degree, is the little room, furrounded as they were on every fide by fuch folid fnow, they had to breathe in for fo long a time. I fhall, therefore, confider each of thefe circumftances by itfelf, and endeavour to fhape my reafonings upon it, by obfervation and experiment; thinking myfelf very happy, if I fhall be found to approach the truth, and appear no way tenacious of my own opinion; a thing which anfwers

no

no other purpofe, but that of involving the fciences in darknefs and confufion, and of courfe, retarding the improvement of them.

One of the worft things thefe poor women had to fuffer in the ftable the whole time of their confinement, was the fenfation of cold, which pierced them to the bones, and from which they could in no fort, defend themfelves. I fhall not here enter into a phyfical difcuffion, in order to determine in what cold confifts, and what it is that excites in our fouls that idea which is called cold. It is fufficient that I obferve, that when the direction of the folar rays towards our earth, is moft oblique, and the ftay of the fun under our horizon, longeft, it is then with us, the feafon which is called winter, and in which cold is felt; and that when any parts of our body are touched by another lefs warm body, we fay that fuch lefs warm body is cold. This we may obferve frequently to happen in fummer, when the winds are high, and attended with hail and heavy rains. Our bodies, through the heat of the feafon, ufed to a warm medium, furrounding and touching us in every part, fuffer a fenfation of cold on the leaft abatement of that warmth; though fuch abated warmth, compared with that of the air in winter, is very intenfe; fo intenfe, that in winter, according to Boerhaave, no man, who had been for fome time expofed to the open air, could continue for any time in a room heated to fuch abated degree, without fainting. It frequently happens, that the country people, on coming down from the very cold mountains into the plains, feel the air temperate, and even fometimes warm, whilft thofe who conftantly refide in thefe very plains, complain of being almoft frozen to death. For my part, thefe obfervations are fufficient to convince me, that we call thofe bodies cold, which, compared with other bodies, are lefs warm; though actually warm, if compared with thofe which are lefs fo. Philofophers, therefore,

therefore, finding by experience that as moſt bodies are put in motion, and rarefied by heat, ſo on the heat's diminiſhing, they loſe that motion, and are condenſed in proportion to ſuch diminution, took occaſion from thence to invent the thermometer; and by obſerving the rarefaction and condenſation of the liquor contained in the tube, in conſequence of which it riſes or falls, have endeavoured to meaſure and determine, or, to ſpeak more properly, indicate by means of ſuch riſing and falling, the different degrees of heat and cold. It is, indeed, true that as yet no inſtrument had been found capable of indicating exactly, at all times, the degree of heat in the human body, and that we are ſtill very far from knowing, what, really, are the cauſes which produce in us the ſenſation of cold. For we often experience in our bodies different degrees of heat and cold, the mercury of the thermometer ſtanding in all the ſame height; and this does not happen in one man only, but in many at the ſame inſtant;

as

as it sometimes happens in winter, that we feel a great degree of cold, whilst the thermometer indicates no such thing; and sometimes again we do not feel that cold, which we felt at other times, when the liquor was at the same height. Hence we may reasonably conclude, that there is some cause operating on the human body capable of lessening its heat and producing cold, whose action does not appear to our senses by means of the glass of the thermometer or the fluids contained in it. It has sometimes happened, that no alteration has been perceived in the fluid of thermometers, placed in the hands of aguish patients, in the cold fit, though attended with frequent yawnings, livedness of the lips and nails, paleness of the face; chattering of the teeth, a great infrequency and slowness of the pulse, such a degree of cold, in short, as the physicians call a bone breaking cold; a most evident proof, that the cause producing cold in the body of such sick persons has no action which

the

the thermometer can exhibit to our senses; for we cannot, on these occasions observe the least alteration in that instrument.

Supposing, then, that all these accounts are true, and, indeed, there is no denying the truth of them, it is certain, that, whatever the essence of cold may be, it must, according to its greater or less intenseness and activity, unavoidably produce various and proportionably sensible alterations in the human body; all philosophers, in general, allowing, that effects always bear a relation not only to the causes, from which they spring, and on which they depend, but likewise to the precise disposition of the bodies, on which they operate. Among these dispositions we may, certainly reckon that, by means of which different, bodies are differently affected by the same degree of cold, insomuch that some shall experience no inconveniency when exposed to a degree of it, by which others are terribly affected. The most general degree of heat the human body

in

in a found state, is thirty-two degrees by Reaumur's thermometer, and by Fahrenheits's ninety-two, and the temperature of the air by the first ten degrees, and by the second fifty-two. It is a moſt ſurpriſing thing, that human bodies did not ſuffer the moſt grievous inconveniencies by the cold of 1709, which was fifteen degrees and a half under the freezing point of Reaumur's thermometer, and at the degree of ſal-ammoniac congelation by Fahrenheit's; however, that ſuch numbers were at that ſeaſon viſited by ſickneſs, and ſo many of theſe periſhed by it, can be attributed to nothing but ſuch extraordinary degree of cold. But what is ſtill more ſurpriſing, there are countries, in which men have lived, and generally live in much more intenſe cold, as may be ſeen in a learned diſſertation of Deliſle's, in which he has collected many obſervations made by himſelf and others, adjuſted to his own and to Reaumur's thermometer. In Aſtracan, in 1746, the cold was at twenty-four degrees

grees and a half under the freezing point of Reaumur's; at Peterſburgh, in 1749, at thirty; at Quebec, in 1743, at thirty-three; at Tornea in Lapland, where the French Academicians, who had been ſent to meaſure a degree of the meridian under the polar circle, made ſome ſtay, it fell to thirty-ſeven. Gmelin has experienced it ſtill greater, for in the preface to his firſt volume upon the plants of Siberia, he affirms, that, according to the obſervations made in all parts of that country, even the moſt ſouthern, the mercury in Deliſle's thermometer has been often at two-hundred and twenty-ſeven degrees, which amounts to almoſt fifty-five degrees and a half under the freezing point of Fahrenheit's. At Kirenga, in particular, at four in the morning of the 10th of February 1738, he ſaw it, according to Fahrenheit's thermometer, almoſt at ſeventy-two degrees; and had before ſeen it, at nine in the morning of the eleventh of December 1736, almoſt at ninety degrees

under

under the freezing point; and at eight the morning of the 29th of the same month and year at more than ninety-nine; and, lastly, the ninth of January of the following year, at more than one hundred and thirty. At Jeniseik, at eleven in in the evening of the fifth of January 1735, he saw it sunk to one hundred and twenty degrees and more under the freezing point; which descent of the mercury, says Gmelin, " Stupenda est, et ante nemini ne in mentem quidem unquam venit. Durante hoc Jeniseensi frigore picæ, et passeres a gelu veluti extincti in terram conciderunt, recreati, quoties post brevem moram in conclave tepidum inferrentur, quæ res Jeniseensibus incolis perquam rara visa est. Fama etiam percepi, insignem ferarum multitudinem a gelu rigentem, et mortuum in silvis inventam esse, nec paucos homines in itinere eo die versatos a gelu ita correptos fuisse, ut succi eorum penitus rigerent, atque conglaciarentur." Now who can account for mens being able to

abide

abide fo intenfe a degree of cold, and live, but by the great variety in the conftitution, manner of living, and, in a word, in the difpofition of thofe bodies, upon which the cold is to act. Bonetus relates of Lewis Saladine, that, at the approach of winter, he found himfelf under a neceffity of fhutting himfelf up in his bed-chamber, and there remain with every the leaft flaw in the walls exactly clofed till the return of fpring. What Hafeneftius relates, is ftill more furprizing. He tells us of a man, who having accuftomed himfelf to live conftantly in warm places, in order to fhun every, even the flighteft, inconveniency, thereby became fo delicate, and fo fenfible to the impreffion of the cold air, that he could never afterwards expofe himfelf to it, without experiencing the greateft evils; fo that at laft, he faw himfelf obliged either to remain in bed loaded with blankets, or when he got up, wrap and fold himfelf up in thick furs, to avoid the difagreeable fenfation excited in others,

when

when they put ice to their face or the back of their hands: nay, the delicacy and sensibility of this man were improved to such a degree, that he could not endure the contact of the summer air, so that, even then, he found it requisite to wear furs, and cover his cheeks and eye-lids. It is, therefore, evident, that the different kinds of life men lead, contribute greatly to render them more or less patient of cold; and that it is owing to this, that some put up with an intense degree of cold better than others; so that one man shall be chilled and frozen almost to death, by a degree of cold scarce felt by another. By all this it is evident, that is not so very easy to determine exactly what is the degree of cold, the human body can endure; as, on the other hand, it is extremely difficult to tell in what degree of heat men cannot live, since some bear heat a great deal better than others.

I just now said, that the heat of the human body, according to the observations of of some persons, is generally at thirty-two degrees of Reaumur's thermometer, and ninety two of Fahrenheit's; which degree of heat in the circumambient air, it would be impossible for them to bear. On the other hand, there are many observations to prove, that men have lived in a much hotter air. Duntze observed in the apartment of his learned master, Holman, at Gottingen, the mercury of Fahrenheit's thermometer at ninety-five degrees on the 24th of July 1750. In South Carolina, Lining saw it rise to ninety-eight degrees in the month of June 1738; and yet there died by it but two men in the streets of Charles town, and some negroes at work in the fields; and in the same country the mercury rose one hundred degrees in the month of July 1751. In Syria, likewise, it rose to ninety-eight, and in Senegal to one hundred and three and a half, as Reaumur tells us in the memoirs of the Royal Academy of Sciences at Paris: and according to the most exact observations of Lerche mentioned by Gmelin, it rofe to one-hundred and three degrees and a half at Aftracan in 1746; upon which Gmelin remarks: " Quid quod tepidariorum Rufficorum calor, in quo homines non unum minutum, fed dimidiam, et integram horam morantur, in centefimum, et octavum, quin in centefimum, atque decimum, et fextum gradum cogit, quæ obfervatio in omni Ruffia quovis die repeti poteft." It is, befides, to be noted, that all thefe obfervations were made with thermometers placed under cover from the folar rays, which certainly, if they had directly fhone on the mercury, could not have failed of driving it much higher, and indicating a ftill greater degree of heat. Thefe obfervations put Duntze upon trying, if by many diligent experiments upon dogs he could afcertain exactly the greateft degree of heat thefe animals are capable of bearing. A maftiff fhut up in a room feventyfeven degrees hot, died in fix hours, the

heat

heat having encreafed in that time to one hundred and thirteen. Another dog of the fame kind, put in a room feventy four degrees hot, did not hold out above four hours, the heat encreafing to one hundred and fifteen degrees: a third, but fmaller, put in a heat of feventy feven degrees, was dead in five hours and a half, the heat having attained one-hundred and twenty-two degrees; another fmall dog, weighing fix pounds, placed in a heat of one hundred and forty-feven degrees, died in twenty-nine minutes. Three other dogs, the firft a brown maftiff, the fecond a black maftiff, but younger and fmaller then the firft, and the third alfo younger, with fky-blue ftroaks, being all placed in the fame room, and at the very fame moment, when the mercury in the open air was at feventy-five degrees; the firft died in a little more than three hours, when the heat of the room was encreafed to one hundred and fix degrees; and the third, in little more than five hours and twenty-
eight

eight minutes, when it was encreafed to one-hundred and nineteen degrees; and the fecond held out feven hours, when the heat was one-hundred and twenty-fix degrees. To conclude, in a fugar-houfe, whofe heat was at one-hundred and forty-fix degrees, a little bird died in two minutes, and a dog in twenty-eight, cafting out at the mouth a red, purulent and ftinking faliva. Now nothing elfe can be reafonably inferred from thefe experiments, than what is already advanced, namely, that it is impoffible to determine precifely the greateft degree of heat in the air, in which men and animals can live; as we have demonftrated, that it is equally impoffible to determine exactly the precife degree of cold in which both muft perifh; both depending on their conftitution, their ufual way of life, and their bodies being more or lefs inured to fuch impreffions.

Now to apply what we have been faying to the cafe in hand, if we confider, that our three poor women were inhabitants of

Berge-

Bergemoletto, a place furrounded by very high mountains, in which it frequently begins to fnow in Auguft, and does not leave off until the end of June, and where, befides, the fnow lies on the ground in one place or another the whole year, it will immediately occur, that their bodies muft have been lefs fufceptible of the impreffions of the cold, than the bodies of thofe accuftomed to a lefs fevere climate; and of this we may the more eafily be perfuaded by recollecting, that a vaft quantity of fnow had fallen before the accident happened, fo that they had already felt a great deal of cold, and, in a manner, inured their bodies to that fenfation. They were, befides, in confequence of their laborious kind of life, of a ftout and hale conftitution, and of fuch a habit of body, that, their fibres being rendered more thick and firm, the cold of the external air could not fo foon make any impreffion on their fluids contained in them, and produce that flownefs of motion which great colds produce

in

in some persons. Boerhaave relates of himself, that going in a calash, in the winter of 1709, in company with a surgeon to see a woman, who had broken her legs, they were seized, both himself, the surgeon, and the rest of the company with heavy, and at the same time so pleasing a drowsiness and desire to sleep, that sleep they certainly must, and miserably perish, if, to avoid so great and so imminent a danger, they had not immediately alighted themselves, and made the rest of the company alight, and taken to their legs. The veins of the skin, when touched by the cold air, contract and become of a less diameter; whence it happens that the blood can no longer flow through them, and get back to the heart, with the same velocity and in the same quantity as before. It therefore, flows more plentifully into the vessels of the brain, which are much better defended and secured from the impression of the cold air then the rest, as it cannot easily pursue its journey by the jugular veins,

veins, which are more expofed to the cold, it ftops and gathers in them fuch quantity, as to prefs upon the fibres of the brain itfelf; and this compreffure is fometimes juft fufficient to produce drowfinefs and fleep. But neither the cold, which the three women had to fuffer in their confinement, was fo violent, nor, in confequence of the habit of body, and the life they led, were they liable to be attacked by fuch grievous and fudden difeafes. I fay grievous and fudden difeafes, fuch as apoplexies, obftinate inflammations of the internal parts, or fuch imflammations of the external, as foon turn to a mortification, or in a word fuch other diforders; as a fharp cold is generally apt to occafion in human bodies. Galen, in the fifth chapter of his book, De morborum differentiis, fays, according to the tranflation of Renatus Carterius: " morbi vero frigidi calido oppofiti affectus extremas partes manifefte adeo plerumque obfidet, ut ipfæ emortuæ decidant. At hujufmodi affectus in univerfo corpore iis oboritur, qui fub

H   vehementi

vehementi frigore iter fecerint. Eorum enim plerique in ipfo itinere mortem obierunt; plerique etiam priufquam domum appuliffent, diverforium affecuti femi-mortui et congelidi fub confpectum veniunt. Talis affectus apoplecticis, epilepticis, tremulis, et convulfis multoties accidit. Porro eorum, qui per iter frigore mortem occubuerunt, alii emprofthotono, alii opifthotono, alii tetano, alii congelatione vocata correpti obriguerunt, alii quid appoplexiæ fimile perpeffi funt." A fervant travelling behind a gentleman's coach, in very cold weather, fell off, and was found by his mafter buried under the fnow, on his return back with the other fervants. Some days after the mafter fent a cart to bring him to be buried: but contrary to all appearance, and to the great furprife of the by-ftanders, on taking him from off the cart, they found him alive; the fhaking of the carriage having put into motion his blood, arrefted and rendered almoft ftagnant by the cold, and thus removed the caufe from whence his apoplexy proceeded. In northern countries,

tries, and in paffing over high mountains, it fometimes happens, that people overtaken by a vehement cold, are in a manner fuddenly ftruck dead by it; and on opening the bodies of thofe who have perifhed in this manner, nothing amifs could be obferved, except a great accumulation of blood and ferum in the ventricles of the brain, occafioned by the burfting of the blood, or lymphatic veffels. We read, that two thoufand foldiers of Charles XII of Sweden, perifhed by the great cold of 1709, and remained ftiff like fo many ftatues. During the laft war, the troops in their paffage over the mountains of Savoy and the county of Nice, were often obliged to alight from their horfes, and purfue their march on foot, on account of the exceffive numbnefs and ftiffnefs, which in confequence of the cold they felt in their legs. We are told in the voyages of Martens and of Wood, that fome Englifhmen, who wintered in Greenland, had their bodies for a time covered with ulcers and veficles.

I fhall

I shall not at present undertake to exhibit all the effects, which cold is capable of causing in human bodies, and the manner in which it causes them: for, example, what is observed in the surface of that part of the body, on which the impression is immediately made, as on the hands, feet, nose, and ears, some of which external parts become livid, others pale, others rough and uneven, others less sensible and supple, and therefore less capable of being used; or, what we know to happen in the internal parts, in which, in consequence of the abatement of motion, the humours stagnate, inflammations ensue, the vessels burst, so that the fluids issuing from them, and gathering in places, where nature did not intend they ought, compress the adjacent parts, and impede their necessary functions. These things I shall pass by in silence, because the cold in the stable buried under the snow, did not amount to such a degree, as to make the women confined in it suffer so much. The reason of of the cold's appearing so very sharp to them, was because that the absolute heat of their own bodies lessened considerably, whilst the cold of the circumambient air continued the same; so that they could not but feel it. This absolute heat arose from the motion of the blood vessels, the oscillation of the fibres, the action of the muscles, the stock of the blood-globules, both against the vessels in which they moved, and against each other, from the impellent forces, and from the resistance these forces had to conquer: all which being much abated, the absolute heat could not but proportionably abate; whence the action of the muscles necessary for life being destroyed, the muscles might be said to be at rest. There was wanting, therefore, one of the causes of the motion of the circular and intestine blood. They took but very little nourishment, so that the quantity of new blood generated in them was exceeding small, and consequently the velocity with which it was driven through

H 3. all

all the channels lefs, and lefs the friction and contraction it underwent in them. Nor does it hence neceffarily follow, that upon the removal of the caufe refifting the impreffion of the external air, which continued almoft in the fame ftate, they fhould have more fenfibly felt fuch impreffions, and experienced a greater degree of cold. We may obferve, that we often feel in very foggy weather, the cold more fenfibly, than in ferene weather, though in the latter, the thermometer is lower than in the former. For which reafon, if we confider, that the air of the ftable in confequence of the perpetual dropping of the water, in proportion as the fnow melted, and the excretions of the women themfelves, as well as of the animals confined with them, muft have been extremely moift, we may difcover another reafon why the cold feemed greater to them, and they muft, therefore, have fuffered fome inconveniences from it, though not equally grievous with thofe it has often occafioned, or fufficient to

bring

bring on immediate death. In fact, Mary Anne, besides her being so posted as not to be able to stir in any shape, and worse off then Anne, and much worse off then Margaret, who yet could scarce stand upon their legs, had her thighs and legs œdematous, and her knees and feet little less then inflexible; which disorder, though we may in part attribute to the constancy of their posture in the manger, must, if the facts already related be true, have been more owing to the moist cold with which they were surrounded.

But if this moist cold could not deprive them of life, neither could the smallness of the quantity of nourishment, with which they were obliged for so long a time to put up. This no doubt contributed very much to their leanness, to their weakness, and to the violent pains they suffered in the stomach every time they eat or drank, for some days after they were taken out: but it was sufficient to keep them alive. I have already related

related many facts, from which it may be gathered that food is in some cases not absolutely necessary to the support of animal life. To these might be added many instances in man and beast. We read of a cat, which being inadvertently shut up in a place, in which not so much as a mouse could penetrate, was found alive after thirty one days, almost bald, and extremely emaciated. Redi writes, that a large lizard a cubit, and two thirds long, which he had received in the year 1669 from the coast of Africa, lived in Florence upwards of eight months, shut up in an iron cage without meat or drink. But whether it died of hunger, or of cold, or of confinement, or some other cause, he could not take upon him to affirm. This learned physician, in order to know what grounds there were for Borelli's suspicion that some animals can live upon gravelly earth, and that birds pick up small stones, by way of food, made the following trials, which I shall relate in his own words. " In fact,

" I may

" I may affirm that I have convinced my-
" felf that thefe fmall ftones taken in by
" birds, contribute nothing to their fup-
" port: upon fhutting up a capon in winter
" without meat or drink, it died in five days;
" and other capons fhut up in like manner,
" without meat or drink live but feven,
" eight, or nine days; and on opening their
" gizzards I found in them a confiderable
" quantity of ftones, fwallowed before
" they had been fhut up, and which in all
" their time of fafting were not confumed
" or converted into nourifhment. I re-
" peated the experiment on another ca-
" pon, whom I conftantly fupplied with
" water, and with a great number of
" ftones, which I firft counted, that by
" way of food, he might have, if he
" pleafed, his fill of them; but he never
" touched them, though in the firft
" days of his confinement he drank rave-
" noufly and frequently. Four days be-
" fore he died, he abated gradually of
" his drinking, and at length died on the

H 5 " twentieth

" twentieth day: another capon confined
" in the fame coop, with the liberty of
" drinking, lived twenty-four days. After
" their death I found in their gizzards
" ftones, as I had found in the firft; I
" likewife found ftones in the gizzards
" of fome large wild pidgeons, who hav-
" ing lived without eating or drinking
" fome twelve, and fome thirteen whole
" days, died at laft. A royal eagle held
" out twenty-eight days, in the dog-
" days, without eating. A vulture held
" out in like manner twenty-one; a
" buzzard, eighteen: and yet the eagle,
" vulture, buzzard, and fuch other
" birds of prey, are not fond of ftones,
" no more than many other birds,
" whofe gizzards are not braced up with
" thofe large and ftrong mufcles, which
" we fee in the gizzards of capons, phea-
" fants, geefe, ducks, fwans, cranes, and
" other birds, accuftomed to peck up
" ftones. Animals do not die for want of
" food fo foon as common people are
" apt

" apt to believe. Of three dogs, whom
" I have killed by hunger, some
" held out without meat or drink thirty-
" four and thirty-seven days. A very
" small dog, in the hottest days of sum-
" mer, lived twenty-five days without
" eating or drinking; and would have
" held out much longer, if, spurred by
" hunger, he had not leapt out of a very
" high window. A civet-cat called by
" Castello Messinesee an odoriferous hyæna
" took up ten days to die, and a large
" wild cat twenty. A musk-roe held out
" twenty days. A badger in winter held
" out a whole month. Rats both wild
" and tame, are very impatient of hunger;
" for in the many trials I have made on
" them, I could never get them to live
" three whole days without food. On the
" contrary, land tortoises have held out
" eighteen months, vipers ten; and as I
" have already said, an African lizard
" more than eight, without ever desiring
" to touch any kind of food. But it is
" the

" the nature of thefe three laft animals
" to take no food at all, or very little,
" and very feldom, in winter. In other
" animals their ftrength and age is of
" great fervice to make them endure hun-
" ger a long time. But in many kinds of
" infects it is likewife nature. It is fur-
" prifing how clean and beautiful we find
" the inteftines of animals killed with
" hunger; which ought to be a leffon,
" that a regular diet is the fafeft remedy
" to reftore the vifcera of the human body,
" and fcour its moft winding and intricate
" channels." Van der Wiel fays, he heard from Craanen, that a very fat large dog having been accidentally fhut up in a room in a country houfe, was found alive on his mafter returning to it, thirty-one days after, though very weak indeed, and emaciated; having paft the whole time, without eating or drinking any thing except a moufe or two, fuppofing that mice are to be met with in lonely places, where they can find nothing to live on.

on. We read in Mendoza, that a hen lived eighty days without meat or drink. Gaſpar Reies, in his fifty-eighth queſtion, in which he examines if a man may naturally live a long while without any meat or drink, gives us ſeveral inſtances of people who have lived without drinking, and many of people who have held out a long time without eating. The moſt remarkable of theſe inſtances, is that of a Spaniſh woman, who lived ſeventy-two days in a cave, without having in all that time any thing to ſubſiſt on, as ſhe afterwards affirmed upon oath, except a little rain water, ſucked from her head-clothes, and which ſhe now and then ſteeped into it. We meet with many more inſtances, in the ſecond century of uncommon caſes of the above-mentioned Van der Wiel, printed at Leyden in 1727. Four men, working in a coal-pit, near Liege, and happening to ſtrike upon a very plentiful vein of water, were by its iſſuing in great abundance upon them, obliged to retire to the higheſt,

but

but inmost part of the mine, where they remained twenty-four days, subsisting entirely on the water trickling from an adjacent spring. It is known, how usual it is with the physicians of Naples to recover patients by not permitting them to swallow any thing but simple snow water, with which they make them hold out thirty-days, and even longer. A Sicilian capuchin and Hanchok have cured more disorders than one in this manner. In the year 1755, I attended for two months a phthisical patient in St. John's hospital, allowing him every day but three pounds of barley water, and six ounces of cow's milk morning and evening; in the same manner I cured another in the year 1756; and they are now both of them alive and well. The reader, I think, cannot but conclude from all these experiments and observations, that men to live require very little nourishment, and that in certain circumstances they may live for some time without any at all. Now, as, supposing

supposing the facts to be true, it is proper, by comparing them with others, to endeavour to account for them the best we can, if not by evident, at least by probable causes, and thereby approach as near as possible, the beautiful face of truth; so, availing ourselves of what has been most learnedly observed and advanced by others upon this head, we shall endeavour to shew, that the little snow water and milk taken by Mary Anne, Anne and Margaret, were sufficient to keep them alive.

In the year 1750, Paul Combalusier, proposed the following question in the medical schools of Paris. "Can a man live "in good health, for a long time, with- "out eating or drinking?" And after a rigorous discussion of every argument that could be allowed on the occasion, he concludes, that a man may live a long time, but not in good health, without eating or drinking. The learned academicians of Bologna, being asked their opinion by Benedict XIV. of happy memory, while a cardinal,

dinal, concerning the two following points: the firſt, if a man by the mere ſtrength of nature, can live for months and years together, without taking any kind of liquid or ſolid nouriſhment; the ſecond, if the opinions of Licetus, Reies, and Zacchia, affirming, that he may really live in that manner, and accounting for it by the maxims of the antient phyſicians, are ſolid or not, when compared with thoſe of the moderns; the learned Academicians, I ſay, anſwered one, and the other by an excellent diſſertation intitled, *De Longis Jejuniis*. For this treatiſe, we are chiefly indebted to the late Matthew Bazani, and Giacomo Bartolommeo Beccari; of whom the learned and holy father makes honourable mention in the following words in his treatiſe: " De ſervorum Dei beatificatione, et beatorum canoniſatione, Part 1. lib. 2. c. 27. Præ ceteris academicis, Jacobus Bartholomaeus Beccarius medicus clarus, et Matthæus Bazanus, philoſophus doctus, medicus probatus, anatomicus non vulgaris, et undeque dequaque difertus in concinnanda differtatione laborarunt.". In this differtation, they prove, firft, by many obfervations on the bodies of men and beafts, that the latter can live a long fpace of time without taking any kind of food; and by fure and certain accounts, that many perfons have actually done fo. fecondly, they confirm this their doctrine taken from the ancients, by the phyfiology of the moderns. Let us now, then, fee what are the grounds of the opinion, that man can live a long time without food; and apply them to the three women in queftion.

Whoever confiders with the leaft attention the component parts, and the operations of the human body, muft allow that they confift entirely of channels, of humours that run in thefe channels. Thefe confift of folid parts, which put in motion, are the principal caufe of the perpetual circulation of the fluids. The life of man, therefore, confifts in the action and re-action of thefe folid and fluid parts, which
cannot

cannot but move reciprocally, and refift each other. The fluids driven into the channels of the human body, cannot but dilate them, and thefe veffels forced out of their natural ftate, cannot but endeavour to return to it, and in fo doing, comprefs and drive forward the contained fluids; as we fee happen in the blood, which driven by the heart into the arteries, is by thefe pufhed into the veins, from whence it flows back again to the heart. This perpetual motion of both fluids and folids, renders the humours more fluid and fubtle, produces the fecretions and excretions, and a violent friction againft the fides of the veffels, from which, of courfe, fome particles muft feparate, efpecially at the extremities of the conic veffels, in which this friction is exceedingly great, the fides being there touched by almoft every globule of the fluids that paffes them. From all, fly off fome very fubtle, moveable, active particles, by fome called fire, by others æther, by others again,

again, electrical matter, from whence arises that heat which diffuses itself all over the body. Now what must be the consequence of this continual action and re-action, but that the channel coming to be gradually worn away and consumed, by the constant flow of the humours through them, and the humours themselves to be dispersed and dissipated by continual exhalation, the human body should in course of time be destroyed, if the remaining humours were not as constantly recruited by new humours, and the channels repaired by an accession of new particles, instead of those carried off by the humours. Now this can only be effected by the taking in of some substance capable of yielding chyle, which mixing with the blood, may enable it to repair all the losses occasioned by continual motion. Wherefore, were it not for the exhalation of the humours, and the abrasion of the channels, both might continue to play and move, without the accession of any foreign matter, and men,

of

of course, to live without the assistance of food. Furthermore, could the humours, notwithstanding the perpetual action and re-action of the fluids and solids, continue in their natural state, and not spoil, man might not only live without food, but enjoy good health. Hence it is, that, according to the difference in point of climate, season, age, constitution, habit, and way of life, we see some persons require a greater, and others less quantity of food; the channels in some, continuing for a long time soft and supple, and the humours sweet and mild; whilst in others, the solid parts soon grow stiff and hard, and the fluids, sour and corrosive. Those who live in a thick heavy air, can better bear remaining for some time without any food, than those who live in a thin light air. In summer-time, on account of the increased motion of the blood, and exhalation of the humours, we should eat and drink more frequently, in order to replace the particles of the body which fly off in that season, fon, more than in winter, in which we perfpire lefs, and lofe lefs by the pores of the fkin, which are greatly contracted by cold. Youths and boys, generally fpeaking, (what I fay in general, in regard to different feafons, and different ages, is to be underftood of different conftitutions, and all the other differences I have mentioned) youths and boys, I fay, generally fpeaking, are obliged to eat and drink much oftener, and in much greater quantity than grown up people, as well as perfons far advanced in years, and fuffer much more by the want of nourifhment. "Inediam (Celfus obferves) facillime fuftinent mediæ ætates, minus juvenes, minime pueri et fenectute confecti." Such bodies as have foft, and not very elaftic fibres, and abound in humours, do not ftand fo much in need of frequent nourifhment, as thofe whofe fibres are ftronger and more elaftic, which drive on the humours with more violence, and attenuate them to a greater degree, fo as to render

the

the dispersion of them more copious. It is for this reason, that women can much longer do without food than men. Every one knows the force of custom, which physicians call a second nature, and to which the greatest regard and attention is to be had in the cure of disorders; it being certain, that those things to which we are not accustomed, do us more mischief than those to which we are; though the former are in themselves more wholesome than the latter, and more suitable to our nature. He who has used himself to live upon little, may hold out without that little, some time longer than a person used to eat more. Pechlin gives us an account of a tapestry weaver, who took no food but twice a week, without receiving any hurt from so long an abstinence. Those who have accustomed themselves to very little food, do not miss that little, if they chuse to do without it. To conclude, we observe that persons of a sedentary and delicate way of life, such as do not too much fatigue either body

body or mind, and who live on very fucculent and nourifhing things, can bear being longer without any food, than country labourers, artizans, and fuch people who fpend the whole day in bodily exercifes, and ufe a coarfer and lefs chiliferous diet. " Ubi fames, minime laborandum eft," fays Hippocrates: and Celfus; " Si quibus de caufis futura inedia eft, labor omnis vitandus eft." It is obfervable, that thofe who fleep a great deal, are not apt to have good appetites; and that, on the contrary, thofe who fleep little, require a proportionably greater quantity of food. That great philofopher Bacon, affirms: " Animantia fomno plurimum indulgere folita, modico victitare, ut glires, vefpertiliones." We have in Reaumur's memoirs of infects, a very curious obfervation communicated to him by Varignon. Varignon had a dormoufe, who ufed to fleep fo foundly in winter, that nothing lefs than the heat of a lighted candle could awaken him, relapfing into his profound fleep as

foon

soon as the smart, occasioned by the candle was over. One Chilton, as we are told in the philosophical transactions, used to sleep for several weeks together, and though he sometimes, during these fits, eat and drank in a strange and unusual way; at other times, he either took no sustenance, or took it very sparingly. William Foxley, a potter, as Wiel has related out of the annals of England, in the reign of Henry VIII. was seized, without any previous distemper, with so heavy a sleep, that he shewed no appearance of waking fourteen days and fifteen nights together; and when he at last awoke on the fifteen day, he awoke in perfect health, and in so firm a belief, that he had slept but one night, that nothing but the building of a neighbouring wall could convince him of the contrary. It being therefore plain, from what has been said, that the action and re-action of the humours and channels of the human body, may be so abated, as that it shall not decay by little nourishment; we may, I fancy,

I fancy, the more eafily conceive, on examining into the condition of the three women buried under the valanca, how with the little fnow they ufed to put into their mouths, and the little milk their friendly goats fupplied them with, they might have held out, though with difficulty and detriment to their health.

The chief things which oblige men to eat and drink, are motion, exercife, and fatigue, which increafes the attenuation and difperfion of the fluids, the abrafion of the channels, and that heat which difufes itfelf over the whole body, and which, at the fame time that it is neceffary for the prefervation of the human body, tends to deftroy it, not only by greatly diminifhing, condenfing, and fouring the remaining fluids, but likewife by encreafing the rigidity of the folids. From the three women continuing conftantly motionlefs in the fame pofture, we may conclude, that their humours muft have moved with far lefs velocity than ufual; that the abrafion of the

fides

sides of the channels, must have been far less; that the heat of their bodies, and, of course, the attenuation and evaporation of their humours, must have greatly abated, so as considerably to lessen the necessity of taking any nourishment to repair the losses sustained by channels and humours. Where there is no waste, there can be no necessity for repairs. Besides, some are of opinion, that in cases where no new sustenance can be taken, great help is derived from the humours which have not as yet been thoroughly digested, of which there constantly remains some portion, particularly the fat, to supply the place of what is lost; though the observations made upon frogs and bears, which come fair and fat out of their holes and dens, leave some room to doubt, whether in those animals, which pass the winter motionless, and almost constantly asleep, the fat is intended to yield them any great support. Be that as it will, the separations and excretions,

which

which are conftantly going forward, require that the body fhould take fome new nourifhment. Now thefe functions were remarkably diminifhed in the three women, and fome of them, efpecially in Mary Anne, totally fuppreffed. There, therefore ceafed in them another caufe of our taking nourifhment, fo that the little fnow and milk they now and then took, might very well repair the fmall wafte their bodies fuffered.

Hence it appears, that the moft wonderful part of thefe womens ftory, is not the great cold they endured, nor yet the fmall quantity of nourifhment they were obliged to put up with. The moft furprifing circumftance of it, in my opinion, is their not having immediately perifhed for want of air, as what they had, could not, at firft fight, but foon lofe, by breathing it fo often, its power to extend and work their lungs. By the havock the valanca made, as well as by the fpace it occupied,

pied, it is evident that the snow, under which they lay in the almost ruined stable, must have been very high and thick. It was, in fact, as I have already said, forty-two feet high. The space found free, when they were dug out, was six feet long, four broad, and two and a half high. It is true, that in the beginning, this space might have been larger, but it grew less and less from day to day, through the settling and greater condensation of the snow. Besides, this prison contained two goats, who could no more live than the women without a supply of fresh air, and from whom too, there must have escaped by insensible perspiration, some very small particles, though perhaps in no great plenty. Besides, there could not but arise many effluvia from the dead bodies of the boy, the ass, and the hens, which along with those from the excrements of the women and the goats, could not but render the air of the stable unhealthy, and ill qualified

to

to favour the indispensably requisite business of respiration. Who does not know, that the air of prisons, into which numbers are crowded, is greatly infected by the constant exhalation from their bodies, which have so few and small openings to escape at. Much worse still is the air of hospitals, on account of the great quantity of unwholesome effluvia exhaled by the sick, and their continually breathing their own breath; the smell felt on entering, being such, that to characterize any bad smell, we call it an hospital stench. What bad effects such air is apt to have, those can tell who serve and attend the sick, and pay so little regard to their own health and that of the patients, as to take no care to mend it. It is for this reason, that following the useful and laudable instructions, given in our university, and in the hospital of my most learned and friendly master doctor Badia, physician to his majesty, I have given orders, that in the hospital of St. John,

what-

(whatever the incurables, who know not their own good, may think of it) every morning, even in winter, the windows should be thrown up, and left open in that ward where it is my lot to attend, by which means, the poisonous vapours accumulated in the night time, are driven out and dispersed, and new air, fitter for respiration, introduced, to the great advantage of the sick, my scholars, and myself. What we thus see in hospitals, we may observe in proportion in private houses, whose inhabitants sometimes experience, to their unspeakable detriment, how unwholesome it is to keep the curtains of the sick man's bed always shut, the rooms too close and warm, and the sick themselves, loaded with blankets; as is the custom of some, especially in the small-pox, and in many fevers, which it is too usual to consider as miliary fevers. " Vidi ego", says Huxham, " Multoties anxietates, et languores febriles momento fere depulsos, fenestris
tantum

tantum apertis, quibus imprudens nutricula fpiritibus, uti dicitur, volatilibus perperam omnino mederi fatagit; immo tunc adeo non juvant cardiaca calidiora, ut etiam maxime noceant: longe enim melius refpiratione auræ frigidæ, et miffione nonnunquam fanguinis abiguntur: quia ortum habent fæpiffime a congeftione, et nimia fanguinis rarefactione in pulmonibus." Thofe too, who work in deep and clofe places, experience the fatal confequences of breathing the air generally contained in fuch fituations. The precautions taken by fextons and the like, to keep the graves open for fome time before they go down into them, fhews that they know that the air pent up in thofe places, is very pernicious. Cuftom, I muft own, is very powerful in thefe cafes; for the Europeans who go to certain parts of America, fuffer much more in the beginning from the climate, than they do when they have been for fome time accuftomed to it.

In Boyle's " Nova Experimenta pneumatica refpirationem fpectantia," we have an account of four experiments, made by him, on a moufe, to fhew how powerful ufe is, in qualifying animals to live in an air deprived of its elafticity, and thereby rendered in a manner unfit for refpiration. He put a little moufe into a round wide necked bottle, containing eight ounces of water, with a bladder, void of air, tied over it. Then placing the bottle under a middle fized receiver, to which was fitted an exact barometer, he began to extract the air, till he judged he left behind but one fourth part of what the receiver originally contained. The bladder, upon this, fwelled with the air rarefied in the bottle to fuch a degree, as to appear about half full; and the moufe, panting, endeavoured, to efcape by the mouth of the bottle. Fearing, therefore, it might die, he let new air into the receiver, upon which the bladder

imme-

immediately fubfided to its priftine ftate, and the moufe recovered itfelf. Having let it reft a little, he again exhaufted the air to the fame degree as at firft, notwithftanding which, the moufe made no attempt to get out of the bottle for four minutes; but at the end of this fhort fpace, it feemed to be ill again, and therefore Mr. Boyle, once more, let new air into the receiver. The moufe, upon this, recovered a fecond time, but with great difficulty, trembling all over, and for a long while unable to ftand. Willing, however, to make fome further experiments on the creature, Mr. Boyle again placed it in the fame manner under the receiver, and after he had extracted the air to the fame degree as in the proceeding experiments, which appeared by the barometer and the fwelling of the bladder, the moufe continued a whole quarter of an hour without any apparent danger of dying. The accurate Englifhman even obferved, that when in this experiment the creature was put all trembling under the receiver, the trembling went off, though the air had been almoft intirely exhaufted out of the receiver, and of courfe the decanter; that it did not tremble again, but returned to itfelf much fooner when the bottle was taken out of the receiver. To conclude, he placed the moufe for the fourth time and in the fame manner under the receiver, and exhaufting the air, till the mercury had funk half an inch lower than in any of the preceeding experiments, the moufe appeared a little affected by it in the beginning, but foon grew quiet again, and remained fo for a quarter of an hour; at the end of which, Mr. Boyle being defirous of feeing what effect a greater rarefaction of the air might have on it, he began to work the pump once more, and made three ftrokes before the creature fhewed any figns of being in imminent danger of death. As foon as it did, he let in new air, on which

the

the little creature took breath and recovered again much sooner than he could expect. The most singular circumstance of these experiments, in making of which Mr. Boyle does not tell us what time he employed, is that he never took the bladder from off the mouth of the bottle, so that the creature must the whole while have breathed the same air. After all, Boyle in the conclusion says, that though he lays no small stress on these experiments, he is, notwithstanding, obliged candidly to own, in consequence of one or two afterwards made by him, that to affirm any thing positively concerning animals being able to accustom themselves to breathe such air, the same experiments should be made again and again, and on different kinds of animals. On the other hand, Desaguliers has likewise observed, that some kinds of animals reduced by certain pernicious vapours to the last gasp, and then recovered, suffer less from these vapours if exposed to them a second time,

time, nay, sometimes suffer nothing from them at all.

Many and very different are the opinions of physiologists concerning that property of the air in consequence of which, when frequently breathed, it gradually loses its wholesomeness, and its power to dilate the lungs to the degree requisite for the support of life. Some have believed, that, among the great number of particles of different kinds contained in the circumambient air, which we alternately draw in and throw out again, there are some, which, reabsorbed or reimbibed by the humours through the external surface of the body, or insinuating themselves into the blood itself by means of the lungs, are very fit to nourish the body. Nay, some look upon these particles to be so necessary in this respect, as to attribute the death of animals shut up in places having no communication with the external air, to nothing else but the total consumption of such particles

cles in the air contained in the body, and the want of a new fupply. Others have thought, that, in thefe cafes, the death of the animals is owing to the exhalations of their own bodies, which, not being carried off by an acceffion of frefh air, continue to furround them, and acquire fo pernicious a quality, as when taken in again to occafion death. Some, to conclude, do not attribute the death of thofe animals either to the failure of nutritious particles in the air, or to the poifonous quality of the ftagnant exhalations, but to the air's lofing that determinate degree of elafticity requifite to expand the veficles of the lungs, not only in confequence of its paffing and re-paffing fo often through thefe organs, but likewife by the accumulated effluvia of the bodies themfelves.

From thefe three principal opinions, one may, I think, reafonably conclude, that

that when many animals are too closely shut up in the same place to have any communication with the external air, they must die much sooner, than a single animal in the same circumstances. This consequence, however, is not relished by the learned doctor Pistorini, who in contradiction to all the three opinions, affirms, that having shut up two birds in a place that had no communication with the open air, he saw them die in the same time, in which two others of the same age and kind died in different places. Great difficulties, no doubt, arise from these experiments against the three foregoing opinions. Of this, among others, was aware doctor Verrati, who willing to see if the thing really happened as Pistorini had related it, made some new experiments with very great exactness; carefully noting the height of the mercury in the barometer, the

degrees

degrees of heat indicated by the thermometer, and the capacity of the veſſels, in which he ſhut up the animals he made his experiments on. The veſſel he made uſe of in his firſt experiments contained two-hundred and ſixty-five cubic inches of air, Paris meaſure. He began by a pigeon, which of theſe two-hundred and ſixty-five cubic inches took up ten, ſo that there remained for the air two-hundred and fifty-five. The height of the mercury in the barometer, was twenty-ſeven inches and nine lines, and in Reaumur's thermometer about twenty-three degrees above the freezing point. Having put the pigeon in the veſſel, and placed the latter with its mouth downwards on a ſmooth and level plate of metal, that the brim might lie the cloſer to the plate, he luted it all round ſo well, that no air could poſſibly get in. In leſs then half an hour the pigeon began to breathe hard and quick, and, this hardneſs and quick-

neſs

ness encreasing by degrees, it died in an hour and three quarters. The day following he took two other pigeons of the same age, and, as well as he could guess, of the same strenght, and placed them in the same vessel he had done the first, on the same plate, and luted it all round in the same manner, with the degree of heat and density of air likewise the same. One died in an hour and thirty-five minutes, and the other seven minutes after, that is to say in an hour and forty-two minutes. By these experiments it appeared to Veratti, that two animals shut up in the same place, and breathing the same air die much sooner than one. However, not satisfied with these experiments on pigeons, he repeated them on other animals, adapting, in them, the vessel to the barometer in such sort, that no alteration in the height of the mercury could be attributed to any thing, but an alteration in the density of the air; breathed

by

by the animals. He put a marten into a veffel, containing about forty cubic inches of air; the mercury of the barometer ftanding at twenty-feven inches and eight lines, and that of the thermometer twenty degrees above the freezing point : in a quarter of an hour, the mercury in the barometer funk three lines, and the bird began to breathe hard. It funk two lines more in the fecond, and three in the third quarter of an hour. In the following half hour it funk four lines more, the marten declining faft, till it died, which was five minutes after, when the mercury had funk a line and a half lower. Thus then the marten lived an hour and twenty minutes, in which time the mercury in the barometer funk an inch and half a line. He then put two martens together into the fame veffel, upon which the mercury funk in the firft quarter of an hour five lines; in the fecond, three, and in the third but two lines; by which time both the birds were

dead;

dead; one dying in half an hour, and ten minutes, and the other at the end of three quarters of an hour, when the mercury was fallen ten lines. He next put three martens into the same veſſel, one of which died in half an hour; the ſecond in thirty-two minutes, and the third in thirty-five; the mercury in the barometer ſinking eight lines in the firſt quarter of an hour, three in the ſecond, and one line in the five laſt minutes, in all one inch. He made the ſame experiments on ſparrows, and ſmall quails; and conſtantly found that one of theſe birds always held out longer than two, and two longer than three. The ſymptoms were nearly the ſame in all theſe birds; a frequent, weak and difficult reſpiration in the beginning; then frequent and ſtrong; and when they were near their end, ſtrong, but a great deal leſs frequent. On opening their little bodies, he could diſcover nothing amiſs, except that the lungs were very red, full of
blood,

blood, and floated in water (a thing not observed by others, who have tried whether the lungs of birds, that have died in vacuo, swim or sink in water, for they always found them to sink) and yet neither hard nor consistent; as they are sometimes found in persons who die of inflammations in these organs, which I have often seen go to the bottom in the course of my anatomical observations on the bodies of hospital patients, that happened to die of that disorder. To conclude Veratti resolved to try, if what he had observed in birds, would hold good in frogs; but he found it was very far from doing so. A frog put into a vessel containing forty-eight cubic inches of air, lived almost three whole days. Of two frogs placed together in the same vessel, one lived five days, and the other eight; and of four, one died the fifth day, and the other three the eighth. The frog, therefore, is the only animal, in which Veratti experienced,

what

what Piftorini fays he obferved in birds; that is, frogs do not die the fooner for being confined more than one at a time in the fame place, not communicating with the external air. For this reafon, Veratti has wifely contented himfelf with concluding that nothing more can be reafonably inferred from the event of thefe experiments, than that live animals confined to a place not communicating with the external air, caufe a diminution in the elafticity of the air left them, and cannot live long in it, whatever may be the occafion of their death.

Now, to return to our own cafe, it is evident from all the foregoing experiments, that the air of the ftable, in which the three women were fo long buried, muft have loft its elafticity, fo as to be no longer fit for refpiration, had it not fome communication with the external air, or recovered its loft elafticity by fome other means. It is a common notion

tion, that air penetrates every where; but whether or no it could make its way through a heap of fnow forty-two feet high, of fnow rolled down from a high and fteep mountain, and encreafed and accumulated to fuch a degree as to overwhelm fo many houfes: whether or no, I fay, air could make its way through fuch a heap of fnow, and of fuch fnow, and make its way in a fufficient quantity to enable the air of the ftable to dilate the lungs of the women enough for them to live, is a queftion I by no means intend to decide: for I think, that from fome experiments made laft year and repeated this, I can point out in what manner the ftable might have been fupplied with new air. The reader may remember, that thefe women ufed from time to time to melt fome fnow in order to drink it, and befides, fwallow fome of it unmelted. He may likewife remember, that from the ill-joined and crazy roof there conftantly diftilled fo much water, that in

fpite

spite of all they could do, their clothes were in a manner rotted by it. Now, this water could be no other than that of the superincumbent snow which was continually melting, and in melting continually discharged a quantity of fresh untainted air, capable of mixing with that of the stable, so as to serve for the respiration of the women and the goats. Wherefore, in order to see if there is a greater quantity of air in snow than in the water produced by it, I made the following experiments, in company with that able naturalist and mathematician, Alessandro Vittorio d'Antoni, major of the regiment of artillery, and director of the royal military schools.

I took two large glass bottles of the same size with long and wide necks, like that expressed table II. fig. 1. and filled them both brimful with snow fallen that morning; with this difference, that the snow in one was rammed down, as hard as I could,

with

with a round piece of wood, whereas that in the other I left juft as I found it. Round the neck A of each, well fmeared with melted fuet, I bound very tight with a fpago, a frefh hog's bladder B, in fuch manner as to make both bladders equal, and effectually prevent any air from entering into or out of the glaffes. Before I tied the bladders on, I emptied them thoroughly of air, and faftened them on in that condition, drawn out and flattened, fo that if any air happened to difengage itfelf from the melted fnow, it could not but fwell them, and thereby evidently prove, that there is more air contained in fnow than in the water yielded by it. This was the fixth of January, 1757, about nine in the morning, the air of the room in which I put the fnow to melt, being, by means of the fire in it, heated two degrees and a half, by Reaumur's thermometer, above the freezing point; whilft the external air, by a thermometer of the fame kind, expofed

to

to the north, was three degrees under the freezing point. As to the barometer, the mercury stood at twenty-seven inches, one line and a half. I placed the two bottles near the chimney, that the snow might melt the faster; and at the end of twenty minutes, I could observe the snow to give away, and both the bladders swell, with this only difference, that the loose snow melted sooner than that which had been rammed, and the bladder bound over the top of the former, swelled less than that bound over the latter. The snow on both bottles was compleatly melted at noon, when both bladders were considerably swelled, but still with this difference already noticed; the bladder bound over the top of the rammed, being more swelled, than that bound over the loose snow. I now put out the fire, and left the bottles the whole evening in the same room; in which the heat by the thermometer continued at two degrees and a half above

the

the freezing point, and the mercury of the barometer likewife at the fame height till three o'clock. Towards the evening the two bladders were a very fmall matter lefs fwelled, than they had been at noon, fo that they ftill evidently contained no fmall quantity of air, of which before the melting of the fnow, there did not appear the leaft fign in them. At half an hour after fix in the evening, I placed the two veffels without the window, expofed to the free and open air; the weather, by a thermometer placed in the fame fituation, being at three degrees and a half under the freezing point, and the mercury of the barometer twenty-feven inches, and two lines and a half high. I did this to difcover by the cooling of the air, whether the fwelling of the bladder might not be entirely owing to the extraordinary heat of the room, in which I made the experiments. I left them in this fituation till half an hour after ten, when the weather, by the thermometer, being four degrees and a half below the

freezing

freezing point, the bladders were a little subsided, though not so much but that I could still perceive a great quantity of air in them, enough to prevent my reducing them to the small space they occupied, when tied to the mouths of the bottles. This expansion still continued greater in the bladder bound over the rammed, than in that bound over the unrammed snow. To this I must add, that in this interval, the mercury rose in the barometer, as I have already said, one line; which is a further proof that the swelling of the bladders, was entirely owing to the air that escaped from the snow; otherwise, on account of the increased density of the air, indicated by the height of the mercury, after the snow's melting increased, the bladders must have sunk into the mouths of the bottles. We may therefore, I think, conclude, from this, and two, in every respect, similar experiments, performed on the fifteenth and eighteenth of the same month, without the least visible difference

in

in the event, that, in the melting the fnow, there efcapes from it a certain quantity of elaftic air, not unlike that which is neceffary for the refpiration of animals.

This therefore fuppofed, I endeavoured to determine by other experiments, in what quantity of this air was contained in a certain quantity of fnow. For this purpofe, I took a wide, but not very long necked glafs recipient, B fig. 2. with three circles or hoops round the external furface of the neck. I weighed it empty, and then full of melted fnow, of which, by that means, I found it to contain one hundred and forty four ounces. I then filled it with loofe unrammed fnow fallen the preceeding night, and weighing it again, found the fnow it contained to weigh but twenty-four ounces. To clofe the mouth with greater exactnefs, I provided a cork, A fig. 3. with a fcrew brim, three inches high, to go over the outfide of the veffel; and that part which was to go into the recipient as deep as the fecond ring, I ordered it to be fmooth. I then made a hole quite through

through this cork, and fixed in it the barometer C. C. C. which I afterwards ſealed ſo well within and without, as to render it quite immoveable. I then ſmeared the brim of the cork, and the outſide of the neck with a mixture of melted hog's lard, ſuet, and bees-wax; and having covered the cork with a dry pork's bladder, rendered ſoft and ſupple with olive oil, I put it into the mouth of the recipient, the bladder reaching below the third ring. Furthermore, that the air eſcaped from the ſnow might neither lift up the ſtopple, nor fly off by the neck of the bottle, by making its way between the ſides of the cork and the bladder faſtened to it, I with a ſpago D. D. fig. 4. tied the bladder round the ſcrew of the cork, ſo tight, and with ſo many turns, that, let ever ſo much air eſcape from the ſnow, it could not poſſibly either lift up the cork, or in any ſhape expand the bladder; but only by being thus confined to the invariable capacity of the recipient, in conſequence of its greater denſity, raiſe the mercury in the barometer.

The

The fourth figure exhibits the recipient ftopt with its cork, covered with the bladder, and tied down with the fpago and the barometer fixed to it. On the firft of February, at nine in the morning, the mercury in the barometer ftanding at twenty-feven inches one line, or three hundred and twenty-five lines, and a thermometer expofed to the open air, being a degree below the freezing point, and another in my room, where there was a fire, two degrees and a half above it; I placed the recipient, full of fnow, and clofed in the manner above defcribed, in my chamber, at fix feet diftance, fideways, from the fire. In proportion as the fnow melted, the mercury in the barometer vifibly rofe, and by the time the fnow was entirely melted, viz. at half an hour after eleven, had got a line and a half above the three hundred and twenty five lines, at which it ftood in the beginning. Confidering, therefore, the twenty-four ounces of fnow, put into a veffel capable of containing one hundred and sixty-four ounces of water, that is, placed in a space six times greater, it is evident, that the snow took up but a sixth part of the internal capacity of the recipient, and that the air which escaped from it in melting, by filling the rest of the vessel, required a space quintuple of that which the snow alone occupied. Consequently, if the air that thus escaped, had but a capacity equal to that of the snow to dilate itself in, it must have continued five times denser, and of course, five times more elastic; so that, instead of raising the mercury in the barometer, one line and a half, it must raise it five times higher, that is, seven lines and a half. Now, dividing the original height of the mercury in the barometer, or three hundred and twenty-five lines by five and a half, the quotient will be forty-three one-third; therefore, in twenty-four ounces of snow, there is about the forty-third part of its volume taken up by air equally dense with that which we breath and live in; and which air escapes in the liquefaction

liquefaction of the snow, besides what remains in the water formed by it.

The third of February, I repeated this experiment on well rammed snow, fallen the preceeding night, with a smaller recipient, containing one hundred and thirty-seven ounces of melted snow. As to the rest, I stopped the recipient with a cork made on purpose, and bound every thing very tight, just as I had done in the first experiment, exhibited by the fourth figure. The quantity of snow thus got into the recipient amounted to forty-eight ounces. The heighth of the mercury in the barometer, was three hundred and twenty-five lines; the thermometer exposed to the open air, a degree and a half; and another in the room, where there was a fire, two degrees and a half, above the freezing point. At eight in the morning, I placed the vessel in the room at six feet distance, as before, sideways, from the fire. About eleven the snow was entirely melted, raising the mercury in the barometer, gradually as it melted, four lines and one twelfth of a line higher than it ſtood in the beginning. So that, the whole capacity of the recipient, being to that taken up by the melted ſnow, as ſeventeen to ſix, and the air diſengaged from the ſnow in melting, being dilated into a capacity, which is as eleven, if the air thus eſcaped, had been confined to a volume, equal to the volume of ſnow turned into water formed by the ſnow, that is ſix, the riſe of the mercury in the barometer, inſtead of being but four lines and one twelfth of a line, would be in the proportion of ſix to eleven, that is about ſeven lines and a half. The heighth of the mercury in the barometer, was in the beginning of the experiment, as I have already obſerved, three hundred and twenty five lines; wherefore, dividing theſe by ſeven and a half, the quotient will be, as in the firſt experiment, about forty-three; and therefore it is plain, that the air eſcaped from the rammed, compared with that eſcaped from the unrammed ſnow, is

always

always proportional to the water feverally formed by them.

Thefe experiments I repeated in the month of January of the prefent year, on rammed and unrammed fnow, and with the fame veffels clofed in the fame manner, and the refult of all was exactly the fame. On the twenty-fourth of January, I made another experiment on rammed fnow, with the veffel containing one hundred and thirty feven ounces of thawed fnow. When I put the fnow in, the mercury ftood at twenty-feven inches, but by the time the fnow was melted, it had rifen to little more than twenty-feven inches and three lines. I kept the recipient at fix feet diftance, fideways, from the fire in a room, in which the thermometer was four degrees above the freezing point, whilft that in another without doors, was three degrees and a half below it. And to know for certain, if the rife of the mercury might not be owing to the heat of the room, inftead of the efcape of any air from the fnow, I

moved

moved the recipient nearer to the fire, upon which the mercury, indeed rofe a trifle; but, on the other hand, it fell again on my removing the recipient back to the fpot where it firft ftood; and this alteration was, befides, fo fmall, as in my opinion not to deferve the leaft notice, and much lefs prove, that the rife of the mercury is owing to any thing but the elafticity of the air efcaped from the fnow in melting. I placed the recipient in another room, which, according to the thermometer was cold half a degree below freezing, yet the mercury did not fink in the leaft, but continued at twenty-feven inches and three lines, the height it was at when I took the veffel from the fire. Having weighed the melted fnow, I found that it contained but fix parts out of feventeen of the whole capacity of the recipient: wherefore (comparing, as we have done in the preceeding experiments, this denfity with that, which the efcaped air would have acquired, if

confined

confined to a fpace equal to that which the fnow occupied; and expreffing this denfity by feven lines and a half) as the atmofphere, at the beginning of the experiment, kept the mercury in the barometer to the height of twenty-feven inches and eleven lines; fo dividing this number by feven lines and a half, we fhall have for quotient forty-three and one fifteenth; that is to fay, that the air efcaped from the thawed fnow occupies, fractions neglected, the forty-third part of the fpace occupied by the water formed by fuch fnow. On the 26th of the fame month, making an experiment of the other recipient one fixth full of unrammed fnow that had fallen two days before, we found that the mercury, which in the beginning of the experiment was at twenty-feven inches five lines and a half, by the end of it had rifen one line and a half: from whence we may draw the fame conclufion as from the preceeding experiments, that is, that air efcaped from fnow in melting is, in bulk, omitting fractions,

the

the forty-fourth part of the said snow resolved into water. I could not make any more of these experiments this year, as there did not fall any more snow in Turin, except towards night-fall on the 20th of February, and on the 25th; the first in very small quantities, and the second mixed with a great deal of water, by which it was presently dissolved. Now by the meteorological observations I have made during the last seven years, the greatest height of the mercury in the barometer has been twenty-seven inches and ten lines, and the least twenty-six inches and five lines; therefore the quantity of air escaped from the thawed snow, compared with the greatest height of the mercury will be $44\frac{8}{15}$, and with the least $42\frac{4}{15}$.

Now, whether this air mixes with the snow, while that substance is forming, or externally adheres to it in its fall; whether the quantity of this air be greater or less, according to the greater or less density of the atmosphere at the time of its falling;

or

or whether, in fine, it abounds more or lefs according to the difpofition it meets in adhering to, and mixing with the fnow, are things I have not enquired into. It was enough for me to prove evidently, that fnows contains air, and in no fmall quantity, fo as to be thence able to account for Mary Anne, Anne, and Margaret Roccia's living fo long in a place, entirely deprived of all frefh air, except what might in the beginning penetrate through fome long, narrow, and winding paffages, the immenfe heap of fnow under which they lay buried, and did moft certainly penetrate it, in proportion as the weather mended, and the fummer advanced; as is plain by the falling away of the valanca, and the extraordinary loofenefs of that part of it neareft the earth. I have faid, *live*, becaufe, as I have already obferved, they fuffered vaftly in point of refpiration; and the great weight, which from time to time they felt upon their chefts, and which they thought

themfelves

themselves obliged to lift up in respiration, sufficiently demonstrates, that, though the circumambient air they breathed, had elasticity enough to keep them alive, it was not, however, of such a quality, nor in such a quantity, as to be able to dilate their lungs as usual in a wholesome and natural state; and of course raise with equal facility and liberty, the chest containing these organs.

All that now remains to make an end of this discourse, is to give some account of the manner in which they have lived to the present time, and what state of health they actually enjoy. On their return from the baths of Valdieri to Bergemoletto in the month of July, Joseph Roccia, enabled by the charitable contribution of his majesty, and his royal highness the duke of Savoy, built himself a new little house about forty paces distant from that which the valanca had demolished. Here with the assistance of the two loving goats, which had preserved the lives of his wife,

daughter

daughter and sister, and the little stock the two last, himself and his son, could with much fatigue lay up in the summer, they all made a shift to pass the following winter. At the return of spring 1756, Anne and Margaret returned to their field labours; but Mary Anne, by reason of the tremor in her eyes, and the pains in her legs and knees, was obliged to stay at home, and confine herself to the within-door work of the family. As they found it impossible to provide in summer, a sufficient stock to last them the winter, Mary Anne, and Anne, in company with Joseph, set out in a very poor plight from Bergemoletto, towards the end of December, and making, on foot, the tour of Piedmont, by the piteous recital of their long, and great sufferings, excited so much compassion, that they every where met with a charitable reception, and plentiful relief. They came to Turin, where I saw them, the 17th of January, 1757, tired and fatigued with their long and painful journies, but in a good state of health,

health, all to Mary Anne's still complaining of the tremor in her eyes, and a great dimness of sight. Three days after they pursued their journey through the towns, villages, and gentlemen's seats, which they had not yet visited, and at the end of March returned home to see Margaret and John, the only children left of six which Mary Anne brought her husband, and content with the generous contributions their melancholy tale had every where procured them. In April, the three still enjoying perfect health, returned to their usual field-labours, and have ever since continued to lead the same life they did before their misfortunes; and with the same degree of health and strength, all to Mary Anne's sight growing worse and worse from day to day, so as to give but too much room to fear that she will at last entirely lose it.

FINIS.

www.ingramcontent.com/pod-product-compliance
Lightning Source LLC
Chambersburg PA
CBHW031813220426
43662CB00007B/626